THE BOW IN THE CLOUDS
Man's Covenant with God

Other Books by Daniel Berrigan, s. J.

TIME WITHOUT NUMBER

THE BRIDE

ENCOUNTERS

"And this will be the pledge of the promise I am making to you, and to all living creatures, your companions, eternally; I will set my bow in the clouds to be a pledge of my covenant with creation." (Gen. 9:13)

The Bow in the Clouds

MAN'S COVENANT WITH GOD

DANIEL BERRIGAN, S.J.

Coward-McCann, Inc., New York

Sister Maria Josephine Berrigan
1868–1960

FORTEM VIRILE PECTORE
LAUDEMUS OMNES FEMINAM

CONTENTS

PART I

1 The Fall

Adam and Creation

In the Garden of Eden, as Genesis tells us, man had all things. Creation was a transparent sign of God's presence. Material blessings were there in abundance. And all these things were truly themselves, more truly than we can know. They were themselves in a way which radiated their spiritual reality. They were not ambushes or temptations or interrogation points to man. We have indeed no way of knowing the strength of the alliance they set up between man and the Creator. But we do know that when we speak of an ascetical or Christian use of things, we are speaking of something which Adam found a natural and even an easy process. He drew the spiritual content of creation to himself by acts of recognition and love. His "naming" of things was a litany of praise to the Creator—a joyous song for the blessings that lay in creation.

Before the Fall, then, human life was at peace with creation. And this peaceable relation of man to creation mirrored the interior state of man. We might express man's state by saying that his life was not yet a pilgrimage. Man was at home—in God, in himself, in this world. His life was a living possession of good. It included the possession of God by the gift of grace, the possession of his own being by integrity of body, and possession of the material world. And this unity of being and possession gave man a larger existence. It assured him that he was the king of creation.

Of all the gifts that creation offered him, surely Eve was the most radiant. Her joy set up a resonance within his own heart. She was a temporal sacrament of the vision of God. In her, man had the culminating proof of the divine favor. It is for this reason that he could recognize Eve from the first moment of her creation. She had been fashioned from his own body; and so Adam recognized her as he knew his own flesh.

This image of a woman drawn from his side is an expression of the intimate love which unites man and woman spiritually, and is the source of their mutual attraction. When all creation was led before Adam, he "named" them, but the sacred writer adds that he found no one like himself. But when the woman was created and led before him, he knew her immediately: "she is bone of my bone, and flesh of my flesh . . ." (Gen. 2:23).

Adam also knew that with no death intervening, he would see Eve in God, and that he and she need not pass through a dolorous separation in order to see God's face. Adam read in Eve no threat, no sword of tragedy. Their love reached outward without temporal boundaries, to the day of eternity.

No threats about him, in time, or in this world. All creation was man's ally. His "naming" of it was a true reflection of the state of things. All things were for him, and he for God.

This ordered beauty spoke of the situation within man, and of his relation to God. The world was his ally because he was God's man. He could be called lord of creation because he was son. The love of God poured into his being the streams of life signified by the nourishment of the Tree of Life. Man possessed all things in peace because he acknowledged that he had received all from Another. Sickness, malice, death, the providence of God appearing as abrupt enemy —all these lay outside the vocabulary of Paradise.

Within the Garden were all things. Its geographical limits were a symbol of man's inner security under God. He was son and heir. Within these boundaries was all his freedom. As far as man was concerned, Eden encompassed the whole material universe. It included the sun and the heavens and waters, and the outer reaches of space. Outside the Garden was literally nothing, as far as man's desire or ambition would carry him. The universe was his, awaiting his humanizing hand. "Increase and multiply and fill the earth, and make it yours" (Gen. 1:28). Man would fulfill this mandate not by sweat or tears or wresting his food from it, but by the simple and adventurous expedient of being himself. For where the king was, all things were kingdom.

Within the Garden there was no pursuing evil to be fled, no lost good to be mourned. Time was an ascent to eternity —without the violent rupture of death. Within man, an order of love existed. His flesh was his friend. It was taken from the world of nature and reflected, in its integrity, the cosmic order that made human life a paradise. He wore his flesh like the badge of his belonging to time and this universe. "From the clay of the ground, the Lord God formed man" (Gen. 2:7).

Youth, it is said, can never believe that it must die. And in the Garden, Adam was the youth of the race. He could not believe in death because death was literally unrealized; no one had died yet. If Adam's knowledge was clear, exact and experimental, surely its most remote element was: I must die.

It is here that our knowledge of Adam becomes tinged with unreality, in the sense that understanding of him cannot be drawn from experience or from the history of man as we know him. It is almost as though man must think of another race than his own when he considers this immortal one. He has no experience of a spiritual universe to which death is a stranger. After the Fall, on the other hand, death is no merely remote or interesting possibility to man; it does not dwell outside him. It is flesh of his flesh. So an immense distance separates our universe and Adam's, our sensibility and his.

Adam was in love. This is undoubtedly the best clue to an understanding of what we might call the prenatal biography of fallen man. We have in the reality of love an experience of a transforming vital urge—one which carries man outside himself. And we know that love, insofar as it is genuine, is also transforming. The exertion carries with it the reward, and the reward is a person. We do not mean by this that love reduces the other to a possession, or that it merely sheds an interesting new light upon the character of another. But when love is active, the beloved appears simultaneously as other and as self. The other is transformed from stranger to friend, and both the self and the other are drawn out of neutrality toward a heightened intensity of mutual life.

Adam was in love. We know, if we are fortunate, what this means. The power of love is the essential survival of Adam's ruin. To the extent that we have a full human life, we can appreciate what love means. Indeed the measure of our understanding of love is the measure of our being human at all. But even were we to know the meaning of love as Teresa or Francis or Ignatius knew it, we would still be far from the truth about Adam's love.

Even in the case of the greatest men, the state of love is troubled by conflict, by the threat of spiritual anarchy, by consciousness of guilt, by the sense of solidarity in atonement, and the weight of personal sin compounded with the history of sin in the race.

Love among men is a victory won against immense odds. And the very name "love" has taken on an ambiguous connotation—for human love is not always prudent or wise or related to God.

If human love is to come to eternal life—what a struggle! It implies vigilance, care of the senses, distrust of the instinctive heart, the will at times to sacrifice even the greatest of human goods. Indeed, experience of life justifies us in saying that the summons of God may come, not as fulfillment of human love, but as its enemy and destroyer.

With Adam, however, the love of God came as a blessing on human love. God's gifts brought all good things with them. The love of God was literally the good fortune of man. It flowed into man's body and spirit. As it touched and impregnated his body, it brought man the greatest likeness which flesh can have to spirit and still be itself, and still not be in the vision of God. What the love of God will bring man's flesh (as we know man) only after death, the love of God conferred on the Adam in this world—within time.

The grace of God also brought man the gift of integrity. So man's human love did not oppose his love for God. But his flesh was entitled to speak for the spirit; it was integral with it. Man's appetites and passions and senses, far from being mute or castrated, had their own voice, but the voices were consonant with the theme of man's destiny, for God had made man "a living soul."

But when fallen man encounters the reality of human love, the threat of sin is always present. Sin is no abstract possibility to man now, no interesting remote report on another culture, on other men. Inherited sin is rooted in our flesh, as a mutation in a flower. Since we are concupiscent men, Saint Paul can call the power of our appetites simply "sin," since it is the occasion of personal sin, and the birthmark of inherited sin. In his letter to the Romans, Paul writes an extended and anguished biography of fallen man, a biography that concludes not in triumph, but in hope of a healing known only to faith: "Pitiable creature that I am, who then shall save me from the body of this death? The grace of God, in Christ Jesus, our Lord" (Rom. 7:24-25).

Along with the threat of sin, the threat of death is also present to man's love. He knows he must die and that those he loves will die. This thought is a heavy sorrow. If there is any hopeful element in this fate, it lies outside the dolorous reality of death itself, outside the evidence of time and this world. Indeed, the only hope the believer can know is death as the Saviour has undergone it, illumined by His promise of victory.

In regard to death and sin, then, it is true to say that fallen man finds his situation completely reversed from that of Adam. The most remote elements of Adam's knowledge have become the most real to us. The remoteness of his knowledge of death and sin are the measure of the perfection of his being. And the brutal realism of our knowledge of death and sin are the measure of the imperfection of the nature his sin has bequeathed to us.

Man's relationship to woman before the Fall is also instructive for us. With Eve, he knew a union that transfigured the flesh. It must be insisted first of all that this union of persons existed in material nature. This is so true that God implies that if man were deprived of the woman with whom he forms one flesh, he could hardly be himself. For Eve is the fullness of that creation of which man is king. In her, man weds all creation, and accepts as "good" whatever God has made.

In Eve man also weds divinity. Woman is like himself, "a living spirit" radically apart from this world. She alone is another "like himself." As his companion in love, woman is also bearer of the divine to man. For man had wedded Eve in grace. In Eve, in an altogether unique way, the Creator was present in His gift.

In Eve, all man's experience of creation and of the Creator was summed up. In knowing her, he knew the most perfect visible image of God. And both terms must be insisted on. Eve led him further into her mystery through communion, sexual experience, knowledge of the person. And at the same time, she led Adam into the mystery of God, who willed to abide in His gift, and to be discovered there. It was precisely in her perfect womanhood that she was image of God.

Adam and Sacrifice

Was sacrifice necessary before the fall of man? We can read in the silence of Scripture on this point a profound footnote on the nature of man himself. It would seem that in his primitive innocence, Adam was able to bring about the purposes of sacrifice without the need of an external rite. He could, simply and naturally, raise mind and heart to God in adoration and offering of his being.

This was so not merely because all creation was transparent with the image of the Creator. The clear or opaque nature of things depends much more on the spiritual state of man than on any material situation outside man. Much more relevant is the fact that man's interior state of order allowed his being to rise easily and naturally to God. Because man was himself, all else revealed God. He was in the state of grace, without experience of sin, or a history of sin, or inherited sin—a state which our consciousness hardly allows us to imagine. So the idea of sin-offerings, the outpouring of blood in a world that had known no death, would have struck a discordant note in an otherwise untroubled creation.

Man's very being was a liturgy. His presence in this world, as man of love, said to God, "I praise Thee, I bless Thee, I adore Thee, I glorify Thee." The grace that poured into his faculties and emotional life and passions and senses rendered them integral and spiritualized. This life of God in man was man's radical sanctification, and through its energies he served the Creator with ease and constancy.

So the history of sacrifice would seem to date rather from the fall of man than from his creation. Sacrifice, in its most general sense, designates persons or objects for specifically religious use. In this way it dramatizes the nature of God and the needs of the creature, for whom God is all in all. The action of sacrifice also implies, at least in a general way, that there exists a world of "neutrality" toward God, a world in which things are not organically directed toward Him; and this condition of things needs to be corrected rather constantly, lest "the world" come to claim all creation for itself, and eventually man also.

It is difficult for us to conceive of a world in which a specific dedication of things to religious use would be unnecessary. For us, acts of worship are an absolute necessity. Even among Christians, the progression of history has opened a breach in the world—a secular and a sacred order. "Sacred" bread, for example, is prepared for the altar by "sacred" hands—an idea born surely of a less attractive religious sense, since it would imply a separation of work from worship, of weekday from worship day, of laity from cleric. And one notes, by way of contrast, that the early Church—whose worship shows great respect for the functions of layman and cleric consequent on sacramental status —still recognized as valid the gift of man's bread from man's table for the use of the altar.

Community worship among unfallen men would have included rites protected by tradition and transmitted to suc-

ceeding generations. Labor, creative and joyful, would reveal
man as maker and lover. Work would save man from ennui
and frustration and give him a sense of possession of his
world, and would multiply signs and images of God around
man as sources of contemplation and joy.

It seems clear from the Genesis account, then, that
Adam's existence already implied a state of things which,
after the Fall, sacrifice could only hope to restore. Man's will
was one with the will of God. His faculties saw the unity of
revealed and natural truths. To be religious or virtuous was
simply to be himself.

At times, his instinct would lead him to symbolic religious
acts expressive of his existence. These acts would take the
form of libations and gestures of offering, rather than the
immolations of victims, which have a connotation of sin.
For in Adam, spiritual death had not yet overcome man,
and death as restorer would have been meaningless. Im-
molation was not yet the price of holiness. So we conceive
Adam's life as excluding the rhythms of tragedy and loss,
the anguished or painful choices which we know. His humanism was not that of the cross, but of a life "hidden in
God."

At certain times even today, the Church allows herself
the joy of returning to the mind and heart of Adam. One
could signalize as her Adamic moments of the liturgy the
lauds of Divine Office, the Gloria and Sanctus of Mass, the
tonality of the Easter season. These are times when believers
pause, in a context of praise and glory, to recall the Adamic
state of man as restored in Christ. At such periods the emotional content of the Mass loses for a time all emphasis on

bloodletting and takes on the feature of the heavenly sacrifice spoken of by Christ. The hopes of the Church carry her forward in time to that moment when she gathers to drink the wine "new, in the kingdom of my Father" (Luke. 22:16).

It is true also that with Adam, the word covenant would have a far different meaning than it has for man today. To him, covenant was no more than a subsumption of love. It was simply the friendship between God and his man. It did not imply a treaty of peace, but a love of communion. We sense this in the idyllic scene of Paradise. Covenant was conversation, mutual presence, a familiar and holy communion.

Covenant had no need of burnt offerings to recall it or repair it. It did not call for special occasions when the people would gather to renew it, as though friendship stood on unsure ground or were in need of being assured of its genuineness or strength. One senses the fidelity of this friendship in the decree of God to create.

> Let us make man, wearing our image and likeness; let us put him in command of the fishes of the sea, and all that flies through the air, and the cattle, and the whole earth, and all the creeping things that move on earth. So God made man to his own image, made them in the image of God. Man and woman both, he created them.
>
> (Gen. 1:26-27)

And concurrently with creation comes an invitation: "Increase and multiply, and fill the earth, and make it yours" (Gen. 1:28). This would seem to be a foreshadowing of later covenants, and of the blessing promised to the great men of Israel from Abraham to the prophets. The blessing would be reducibly twofold—land and posterity.

But in Paradise the implied blessing did not come as a special mark of favor, or as a gift undeserved by reason of sin. The blessing of God was rather the natural consequence of creation. It was the projection of man into the future, and into all inhabitable space. Man was not to be a passing phenomenon on the earth, to disappear at some fitting moment when a stage of evolution or usefulness was past.

But man was freed from pain and reversals, and set apart by a choice of God, chosen in love. There was no such word of sorrow spoken here in Paradise, as we note in the Hebrew covenant, which rejected a corrupt mass for the sake of a faithful remnant. Adam was chosen simply because he was created, and created in love. With man, the covenant has arrived.

May not one read in the blessing given man at creation a sign of the blessing of grace itself? "Increase and multiply and fill the earth." The fruitfulness of man prepares inhabitants for eternity. His fatherhood resembles God's own, in proportion as it is a sharing of spiritual fecundity that makes man both instrument and channel of life. Men are to father not only the bodies of men but, in a certain sense, their souls also. Man's substance, transmitted to his sons, will give expression to the life of the soul. It will also determine in a mysterious way the conditions under which the gifts of grace will flourish or be inhibited. "Increase and multiply" becomes, in its deepest sense, a command which is also an invitation of divine courtesy. By it man and God together transmit the gift of eternity.

Noe and Fallen Man

The covenant with Adam had been synonymous with his creation in grace. But man fell from the friendship of God, and a new beginning had to be made. Immediately we note a painfully different universe, and the sense of fear and distantness in which man deals with God.

Then, some localized misfortune brought about the saving of a remnant of the people through their leader, Noe. God revealed to Noe that He binds Himself to a special relationship to the people; and they bind themselves, in turn, to Him. It is this mutual agreement, undertaken by the prevenient love of God, that will later create a new reality: "My people."

The two blessings first conferred on Adam are promised Noe once more: "dominion over all things" and "descendants." Through these two, man escapes in a sense the process of death and penury. He gains a sufficient number of images about him to teach him his identity. He can read, through these blessings of family and nature, the glory of God and his own grandeur.

And in the midst of the blessing there runs, like a vein through a living body, the command, "Of the blood thou shall not drink. . . . The life is in the blood, and is the Lord's" (Lev. 17:14).

The prohibition is God's way of saving man from the paganism from which he has once been freed. We must picture the situation of a nomadic, precariously subsisting people summoned from paganism and always in danger of falling away. Under the blood prohibition, a logic of the imagination is strongly at work. The life of an animal is in the blood. But the life of all things belongs to God, Who has created it. When man therefore abstains from blood, he pays recognition to God as Creator of life.

Without this slight exception in man's enjoyment of nature, the people would be in danger of succumbing again to the paganism they had renounced. The command reduces this danger. Imbedded in a larger setting of sacrificial ritual, it is an equivalent reminder of the sovereignty of God. An abstention interrupts the rhythms of pleasure and labor, and offers a few good things of this world exclusively to God.

There is no question as yet of a priesthood. But the crude ceremonial outpouring of blood—carried out by a leader in the presence of the tribe—is in itself a powerful religious gesture. Man's life of ritual worship has begun.

We sense, after the deluge, a new start for man. A corrupt paganism has been swept from the earth. Man has beached on a new world. And as Noe stepped out with his remnant into the new morning, the Creator greeted him, as portent of new favor and a new providence. God will again treat with man in the old manner of familiarity and fatherhood. "Come out of the ark, with thy wife and thy sons and their wives . . . bring with thee all the living creatures thou has with thee . . . occupy this earth; increase and multiply upon it" (Gen. 8:15-17).

The primitive account survives undoubtedly in popular imagination. It nevertheless contains a core of truth. Some natural catastrophe had renewed man and his earth. And the religious history of man is underway. Even though it could be said to have really begun with creation, the life of man in God had been interrupted by a sin which denied man's sonship and plunged a sword of division into his nature.

In the beginning, Adam and Eve had about them the impossibly beautiful aura of a primitive paradise. Still, they came to signify tragedy in personal and social choice. What we owe them is mainly in the order of a possibility which failed. In their lives before the Fall, man reads the divine intention, as it struck against human liberty and was temporarily deflected.

But figures like Noe take up the burden of life as man will always know it. Noe stands for conquest of sin by a nature in which concupiscence has asserted itself. He stands for other things man will recognize—conquest of the natural forces of the world, the laborious task of extending man's culture. But above all, he speaks to us of one who persevered in the life of God, and who offered Him an acceptable sacrifice.

Such rites sum up, in their sensuous appeal of blood, oil, smoke and banqueting, the life of man. His toil, recreation, begetting, death, and hope for immortality, all come to focus here. The community rite also reminds man that the Lord is his God. It tells men that God has made all things in the world; that men too are His creation.

But initiation into blood sacrifice is not the only new element that enters world religion with the survivors of the Flood. For the fidelity of God, manifested in creation, is renewed with a different emphasis.

In the beginning, God had looked upon all things, and found them good. But men fell away, and destruction followed.

Yet the plan of God includes the saving of a remnant. He

destroyed, but He also saved. For if men are evil, God will look with favor upon a few just men, and will save the community for their sake.

God's fidelity outlasts sin. And the parable of His fidelity is in nature. His promise will appear in the epiphany of "seed time and harvest, of cold and heat, summer and winter, day and night," which shall "keep their course unaltered" (Gen. 8:22).

And this fidelity of God will never end. The pedagogy of creation has passed over into a pedagogy of faithfulness which will endure until Abram, and finally be fulfilled in the formal covenant.

But for the period of Noe, the days of creation have passed over into a greater reality. In spite of sin, and with sin a sorrowfully accepted presence in the world, the world of creation has still not lost its power of imaging the mystery of God. Rather, as a changeful parable, it reminds men of the unchanging will of God to give gifts to man.

And all this will endure despite sin. God's Word will never be made subject to man's justice. "The Lord is faithful and just. . . . His mercy endures forever."

Creation is now assumed into a world-wide covenant, and nature becomes the material sign of God's fidelity. This is the connection between the assurance to Noah and the later covenants. "This, God said, will be the pledge of the promise I am making to you, and to all living creatures, your companions, eternally; I will set my bow in the clouds, to be a pledge of my covenant with creation" (Gen. 9:13).

One remarkable sentence in the same passage of Genesis indicates the depths of the understanding of God in regard to the fallen state of man. "Never again will I plague the earth on man's account; all the thoughts and imaginations of man's heart, even in his youth, are bent toward evil. Never again will I send affliction such as this upon all living creatures" (Gen. 8:21).

The resolve of God takes into account all issues. He is in tranquil command of all contingencies. Man, God implies, will sin again. But the word of God is not in bonds to man's moral failures, for His name is mercy.

2 Abraham and the Man of Faith

With the summons of Abram by God, the history of covenant enters a new phase. The choice of God prepares a man for new burdens, and for the creation of a new people. And the call comes abruptly, rending Abraham's former life with a single divine stroke. "Leave thy country behind thee, thy kinsfolk, and thy father's home, and come away into a land I will show thee" (Gen. 12:1).

And the promise? Of course there is one, but we note in what general terms it is stated, in such a way that the response of Abraham's faith is challenged. What Abraham is to leave behind as the journey of faith commences is dwelt upon by God with a kind of holy cruelty. And it is instructive to note that a like enumeration will announce the vocations of the new covenant—"He who leaves father and

mother and lands and brethren for My sake . . ." (Matt.
19:29).

What the believer is to renounce can be clearly stated,
for it is the substance of things seen. But the end of his
journey must be veiled in darkness, for it is the substance of
things unseen. What lies ahead of the man of faith can only
be called "promise." And a promise is not fulfillment, any
more than faith is vision. Indeed, God would not even have
had to remind Abraham of what he was leaving behind;
the heart of man could draw it up. It is the sum of everything that fills that heart.

But man's heart must be emptied if God is to enter it.
This is the law, and the symbol of the emptying of the heart
is a journey, the Exodus of man. The dolorous law had been
promulgated when man fell from God's friendship, in his
expulsion from the Garden. From then on, the call of God
did not usually come to man from within creation; rather, it
demanded of him an abrupt detachment from all things. All
that the heart of man loves, good as it may be, must be
emptied from the heart. The summons of God does not invite man, as it once did, gently and joyfully to walk with
God in a garden. That scene was canceled by the misuse of
the gifts of God.

So from Adam's time forward, the vocation of man has
dolorous overtones of loss, exile and renunciation of this
world. Man's love of God is no longer identified by definition with his love of creation.

These great themes underlie the vocation of Abraham.
From the moment of his summons, he became for all time
the type of the man who is called. And he responded with
such heroic faith that there is quite possibly no greater fig-

ure than he among Old or New Testament saints, as Saint Paul would testify.

If we were to seek for the source of his greatness, we would have a workable clue here, at the very beginning of his vocation.

He set up a structure of faith which the believer can recognize. In Abraham we recognize a faith that is already familiar in many respects, to Christian faith. The Council of Trent has listed the acts by which the unbeliever comes to the beginnings of faith—and the enumeration reads somewhat like a description of the mind and heart of Abraham. Certain vital acts are educed by the new believer—acts of renunciation, of sorrow, hope, patience, and openness to God. And these "beginnings of faith" sum up the believer's change of heart, his response to God's call.

So Abraham leaves all things behind which man might legitimately hope to retain—family, horizons, countryside, the roots of memory, the odor and taste of things in the mind. Without these, he is impoverished in his very manhood. Still, the voice of God demands all: "Leave thy country behind thee. . . ."

So, simply, "Abram went out, as the Lord bade him" (Gen. 12:4). It was a momentous spiritual choice, crucial for all history. This man breaks all earthly attachment, and leaves for an unknown country with his sterile wife, simply because God has called, and has promised a blessing to his posterity. The decision is crucial, and it is creative. The divine blessing, outlawed by sin, had again found a human dwelling, a heart worthy of it.

The very existence of the future, the chosen people, is thus made to depend upon an act of absolute faith. A tangled skein of cross-purpose and revolt, of acedia and world-weariness and despair is set right again, as it always will be set right, by the purposeful love of one man.

Abram went out, as the Lord bade him. So great a figure he was, a patriarch in whose body lay, like an awakened seed, the promise whose fulfillment is the Church!

In his heart lay, like the seed that would conceive Isaac, the seed of faith. Giant of faith, he strides from the Old to the New Testament, and inhabits the heart of Paul, and in the Holy Spirit towers upon the Christian vision. He is the father of all who will submit, and "go out"—and are saved.

So we learn very early in sacred history that God's love reaches out only to those men who have undergone a personal exodus—from lands, possessions and natural love. Above all else, man must renounce a human love that seems in no need of correction from on high. He must disavow the covenant he has made, however ignorantly or innocently, with this world. He must disavow a sufficiency that concludes to the rightfulness of love of this world. "Leave all things" is the preliminary of Abraham's greatness. Without this renouncement, the substance of faith will not be granted him, and neither will a holy increase of faith. And even this beginning of faith cannot be the refinement of the selfishness of this world. It cannot merely baptize selfishness, or give it a new name. It must in fact put egoism to death, and summon man away from it, as from a corpse.

Indeed, all the renunciations of Abraham, compounded and drawn up, are summed up in one: die to yourself. "Yourself" expresses the will to love the things of this world in such a way that they deflect the divine will, or rationalize His will out of existence, or put off decision in His favor.

"Leave all things" is then the parable of an incalculable spiritual journey away from selfishness. What must be left behind is clearly understood. There could be no covenant at all unless man knew what he was called upon to sacrifice. God may slay him, but He will not deceive him.

But what of the journey itself, and what will be man's sustenance on the way? And who will greet the traveler at the end? And what provision is he to take against the future? No matter. Only one thing matters. God will show the way. In truth, He is the way. And that His way may be evident, human means are abandoned. To take them with one is to deny the leave-taking one professed—it is to drag paganism along with one, a ponderous caravan of this world. It is to go through the motions of conversion, while at heart remaining an unbeliever.

"So Abraham obeyed, and it was reckoned justice to him" (Rom. 4:23). St. Paul in a sense anticipates God, and gives Abram a name whose announcement God delayed, a name which was in fact conferred at the moment of his obedience —Abraham. "For he put his faith in God and it was reckoned justice in him" (Rom. 4:3). He received his new name like a stain upon the substance of his soul, like light through its depths. It signified a new character, a vocation —the covenant. It quickened like the seed of a young man in an old body; the child of his old age will now give joy to his youth. And all this seems like a complex parable of his new faith, lighting up its many riches. Abraham's vocation is a call to perennial youth, through the doorway of death. It is a victory whose chief ingredient is defeat.

So great is Abraham's faith, such a source of new life, that its example passes over into mankind. Faith makes of

Abraham the father of all who believe. Such a giant was raised up by faith at the dawn of history. His greatness is such that no one page of God's word will say all that is to be said of him. For God could have defined him all at once, but men could not have understood. Abraham must grow upon the human consciousness, awaiting the accretions of time. For thousands of years, this greatness germinates in the consciousness of Christian and Jew. And this giant of the old covenant is known in his true stature finally, only at the beginning of the new covenant. It is Paul who will give God's estimate of him:

> "I have appointed you father of many nations." He is our father, in the sight of God, in whom he believed, who gives life to the dead, and calls into existence what was not before. Abraham, hoping against hope, believed, so that he became the father of many nations. . . . He did not let his faith weaken. . . . In the light of God's promise, he did not waver in unbelief, but was strengthened in faith. Thus he gave glory to God, by his strong conviction that whatever God has promised, he is able to carry out. Therefore his faith was credited to him as holiness.
>
> (Rom. 4:17-22)

God sent His call to Abram, to that which had no being; and He named him Abraham, because he came to be. The One in whom Abraham believed is the God "Who gives life to the dead, and calls nothingness into being" (Rom. 4:17). And this new creation, this call into being, was simultaneously a response. To be granted the call was a gift; to be granted to hear the call was also a gift. But the gift did not destroy the one who received, or reduce him to a mechanism in the hands of the Giver of life. He remained a man, in that instantaneous mystery by which he arose as a believer, as God's man; from nothingness in God's sight, to a friend of God.

In the eyes of the God Who summons, these things are one—the summons, Abraham's answer, and the gift of faith. It would seem, from the Pauline doctrine on justification, that this is the meaning of Paul's citation of the text from Genesis 15:6 in Abraham's regard. Abraham's faith is not so much the adhesion of his mind to a proposed truth. It is his confidence in a promise which, humanly speaking, is beyond realization. And God recognized and rewarded the integrity of his act. He "accounted it to justice," the just man being one whose submission and rectitude have made him pleasing to God.

The faith of Abraham elicits the conduct of a believer, and the justice of which Paul speaks is of course not merely a "declarative" justice. It is an inner holiness and renewal, a "new creation."

Achieving friendship with God, the true term of his journey, Abraham becomes worthy not only to possess the earth, but never to die. Dying to himself, he achieved eternal life, and life not only among the blessed in heaven, but among men too. For the life which he won by God's gift was a reward which denied him no good thing.

It gave him not only eternal life, but life in this world also. He won possessions and lands, and posterity. He claimed the future; in a true sense, he began the sacred history of the Church. He has become our father.

"He hoped against hope" (Rom. 4:18). The earliest writers of the Church have sought in vain an equivalent for this phrase, encompassing as it does the spiritual greatness of this man. So Chrysostom, "Past hope of men, in hope of God." And Severianus, "Past hope of his own nature, in hope of the power of Him that promised." In Abraham's faith and hope the Church Fathers see a dramatization of the conquest of man by grace. It is as though within one man, identical figures met and wrestled. Their features were alike, but one was according to the flesh, the other according to God. Both were named hope, but one had its feet set in this world; and he would conquer only if he remained imbedded in the earth which had sired him. The other was named hope in God. And the final victory of Abraham was not that he slew earthly hope, but that he overcame and eventually befriended it.

So Abraham believed, hoping against hope, and became the father of many nations. It seems wonderful that men must wait so long before they could understand the full stature of this man. They must come to him by a pilgrimage like his. And it seems fitting that a man of the new covenant, Saul named Paul, should recognize in the Holy Spirit the father of his faith, and should greet him in God's word. For Paul had also undergone a journey out of unknowing into wisdom, and in writing of Father Abraham, was identifying himself as his son—son of the promise, Isaac of the new covenant.

Abraham believed, and obeyed; and his reward was not peace, but greater holiness. The distinction is noteworthy. It is not God's way to leave greatness untried, especially when this greatness is destined to lead other men to God.

"After this, God would put Abraham to the test" (Gen.

22:1). The stroke of God fell upon Isaac, child of the promise, the one who stood in the house as sign that God had
visited his people.

Through his young son, Abraham is now summoned by
God to greater suffering. We are reminded, in the persist-
ence with which God tests the patriarch, of the dangers
which assail faith—the ease with which man accustoms himself to the gift of God. Man is seduced by the things of this
world, the things he fancies he is only using; then he takes
up his life, a reputedly religious being. But how will he
continue to approach the holiness of God by the right use
of this world? The answer is in God, not in man. Man will
grow in the life of God only by a continuing purification
which will enlighten his mind and heart, and teach him
gently and inexorably that if he turns from God to adore
the gifts of God, he is an idolater.

"Take thy son Isaac and sacrifice him to Me" (Gen.
22:2). We sense the abruptness of God, His determination
that Abraham come through suffering to greater heroism.

This new test must be seen in its social aspects. For suffering probes the quality of human life, not only in its inner mystery, but in the relations it bears to other men.

Abraham must be so probed. Is Abraham truly man of
God? Will he lead his people, not toward a materialistic
paradise, but toward God? Is he purified of heart, so that
under the signs of this world—poverty, exile, providential
testings, sin, revolt in the community—he can remain God's
man? Is he marked by steadfastness, evenness of mood and
temper, when Providence remains hidden and painful? In
prosperity, will he take root in this world, as though time
were eternity? In harsh circumstances, will he begin to mur-

mur that the Lord has abandoned him? Or will he hope against hope, under all the fortunes of life, so that prosperity will not rot the fabric of his love, as adversity will not wear it thin?

The first purification was done with. Abraham was fit to be called God's man. He stood before God and did not fear that summons: "I am God Almighty. Live in My sight, and be perfect" (Gen. 17:1).

It is marvelous, even to the believer, that the rewards of fidelity to God are far different in this world and in eternity. In essence, of course, the reward is one. It is the same God Who calls and Who rewards. But the rewards can never take an identical form in time and in eternity, and it is the height of folly to confuse them. In eternity, God will offer man a union and joy which are without end. But in time, He offers responsibility, labors, testing, burdens. God is the victory of man, but not in time. In this world, love wears a face of suffering, and deals out suffering to man. "For the sake of mercy, I have been without mercy to you."

In Abraham's case, the mercy of God fell like a destroying angel on the son of his heart. This is the child out of whose body God has declared that a nation will rise. Of this child God said, before he was even conceived, "Him too, I will bless, giving him whole nations for his posterity; kings with their peoples shall take their origin from him" (Gen. 17:16). And again, with what insistence, lest there be even a lingering doubt of the issue, "It is through Isaac thy posterity will be traced" (Gen. 17:19).

The call to sacrifice reminds believers that the beginning of holiness is not holiness itself. Even if the first summons of God has within it the seeds of the future, and man is firm in his first response to God, still the life of man in God is jeopardized, and many sufferings await man until his faith is worthy of its crown.

A man leaves father and mother and lands and flocks—and he concludes that he has left everything. He has yet to learn that he has left nothing. He has left only the things of a child.

To resign one thing, even for a better one, is not yet to possess God. A first renunciation is the mark of a good beginner, a Christian neophyte. But such a one has not yet merited the name of friend, saint, lover, apostle. These words come to crown a lifetime of sacrifice.

And if there are obstacles against a first response to God, others await the Christian; and after a first stage of belief there will be purifications and testings for the fervent believer; and after that there remains the most difficult stage of all—that of the hero.

These are the things that Abraham discovered. He had traveled that immense spiritual distance which separated Abram the pagan from the believer Abraham. And another dolorous journey was imposed on him. "Take the child Issac, and sacrifice him to Me on the mount Horeb." Short of being entirely God's man, even the greatest of men is not yet himself. His life must stand before God's scrutiny, in an encounter that both invites growth and brings it to pass. Failing this continued openness to God, a holy life will lose its radiant promise. A cloud comes over the memory of that day when God's summons first met the heart of man, and both God and man emerged victors.

With what a sobriety and primitive directness the account of Abraham's sacrifice has come to us! It is free of all psy-

chological clutter. It leaves unfilled those spiritual interstices
which a merely curious mind will wish to enter. One pon-
ders the old man's grief, his hopes endangered, his summons
to the heights of the spirit—a height that takes him all but
out of our sight. But we are left to infer all this, reading between the simple, austere lines of the text. The simplicity
of the account says to the believer: "Blessed is the man who
has learned to suffer."

Abraham suffers, that is, in such a way that he does not
lose touch with reality. He submits to anguish and is able to
search out a point of stillness in which his spirit can declare
that one and the same love had decreed blessing and sorrow.

In the Genesis account, we have no soliloquies, no evidence of inner turmoil. "Rising therefore at dawn, Abraham saddled his ass, bidding two of the menservants and his
son Isaac follow him; he cut the wood needed for the burnt
sacrifice; and then set out for the place of which God had
spoken to him. It was two days later when he looked up and
saw it, still far off . . ." (Gen. 22: 3, 4).

The truly dramatic occurs when drama, as an end in itself
is lost sight of. Life must reveal, through action and motive,
an evidence of greatness that will imply the spiritual mystery
of man's being. There must be no intent to teach, to edify
or to force issues. But a moment of crisis, to which man submits with a dolorous sense of loyalty to the community and
to God, reveals man for what he is. "Take thy son, thy only
son Isaac, and offer him to Me in burnt sacrifice on a mountain which I will show thee."

Hoping against hope, Abraham is praised beyond praise.
The journey continued, for a matter of days, in a spirit of
hope. It was such hope, we are justified in concluding, as

would make the despair of most men seem pale by comparison. It was a hope exposed and without recourse in this
world. It was, even, seemingly without recourse to God Himself, since His own command had put hope to death. Many
hours of solitude along the mountain way allowed the father to recall sorrowfully and lovingly the history of the
child whose hand he held. Isaac was a child of hope, conceived against hope, born out of time, arriving in this world
as a sign of God. Isaac had become, even as a child, the
founder of hope; he was, even as a child, the father of the future.

But now, abruptly, hope is canceled. Hope has become, instead of supremely logical, the absurd. Yet by its depths as
well as by its height, Abraham's trust vindicated itself. His
hope suddenly became itself, when reasons for hope had
vanished. For how shall we say that a man trusts, when he
has before him the fulfillment of hope? If he seeks a sign, or
puts trust in the favorable events of this world—in the
facts that things go well, or that no one opposes him, or that
his life is comforted with material blessings—if he lives in
this fashion, he lives by a worldly hope that has nothing to
do with the darkness of God.

But let human hope be threatened, and then both God
and man will know the equality of a man. Let human life
be threatened in such a way that dramatic irony is left intact—in such a way, that is, that the believing audience
knows a favorable outcome is imminent, but the protagonist
knows nothing, except that the reasons for his hope seem to
have vanished. In such an eventuality, man will know peace
only if he can distinguish between the God in Whom he

hopes, and the evidence which this world, or his senses, or his pride, offer him for hope.

So Abraham distinguished. His heart remained firm in God. He raised his heart above the appearances of things, even above the earthly realities of death and sacrifice, and he "waited upon God." And the magnitude of his greatness lies in the opposites which his hope reconciled. He dared to face both the promise of God and the command which destroyed the promise. On the one hand, he could not but remember God's words: "From thy issue, kings shall rise. . . . It is through Isaac, thy posterity will be traced." And on the other hand, he obeyed. "Take thy only son, and offer him to me in burnt sacrifice on the mountain which I will show thee."

From the obedience of Abraham, one can conclude paradoxically to the greatness of the trust which he had placed in God's promise. If the virtue of obedience is integral, it sustains man's trust. Abraham is like a careful workman who is obliged to keep opposite weights in balance. He dares not add a great weight to one side of his balance without at the same time adding to the other. Or rather, it is God Who simultaneously adds to his burden, and increases the spiritual courage and stature which will sustain man. On the one hand a burden of obedience; on the other, a corresponding and vital hope.

So his trust and his obedience sustain him. But still he knows anguish. Abraham is not an image of Atlas, he is a man of flesh and blood. "Take thy only son, beloved son Isaac . . ." One senses the weight which lies on the heart of the father. His burden is measured by the worth of the victim, and by the state to which the offering will reduce him.

Of the worth of such a son the sacred account says nothing directly. The silence of the father, overflowing with holy anguish, is most eloquent. And in this regard it may be useful to recall the meaning of the burnt sacrifice which God had commanded.

Without anticipating the Mosaic code and its elaboration of sacrifices, one can learn from the nature of this offering why it was destined to hold an eminent place in Jewish worship. It was, in fact, the supreme act of adoration to God, since in it the whole victim was consumed by fire on the altar and no part of it fell to the use of man. In later Mosaic law it became strictly a priestly function. No layman or Levite was allowed to approach for the essential part of the rite—the arranging of the victim, the supervision of the firing, and (where this occurred) the sprinkling of blood on altar and people.

The ritual of burning was an essential of the sacrifice. It expressed, in as absolute a manner as possible, the dominion of God over His creation. In fire, the whole victim seemed to rise to God as a symbol of the ascent of the believing community. So the holocaust expressed the profound spiritual decision of the community to put to death its collective selfishness and pride and lust, and to live to God. The sovereignty of God over the things of this world was asserted in an ascending dramatic image. To God, man conceded dominion over the human spirit: over private and social decisions, over public and secret acts. And on man, in turn, God bestowed a kingship relieved of the slavery of misuse and passion and fear. Through sacrifice, man became a noble steward of God.

Now the gift offered to God becomes a more powerful symbol of the death offering of the community, in proportion as the object offered approaches a resemblance to man, or is deeply loved by him. Indeed, the only gift fit to be offered at all is something greatly loved by man. The law itself implies this in designating the choicest victims for the burnt sacrifices—the first fruits, the unblemished fruits.

But in Abraham's case, we understand that the sacrifice demanded by God is no mere object. It is a very person. The victim is not led dumbly to the altar, a heifer or a lamb. The victim is the loved other, the person.

If among all civilized men, the stranger at the door is a sacred trust, what shall one say of the child of the house? In sonship, the mystery of the person takes up its dwelling under man's own roof, in his very heart. Sonship is the extension of the spirit of man. The flesh has generated the flesh, man has declared his kingship over creation in the power of generation. He has produced another like himself to continue his tasks within time, to restore his failing years, to project order into another generation.

But this of course is only a part of the truth. A son represents not merely mastery over this world and an extension of its processes in time, but simply a mystery. Man knows that in sonship, he has brought forth another who will see the face of God. The child is in this sense a reminder of that ideal era which man knew before the Fall. In his son, he may read again the unmarred power of love to invade eternity by the power of love. For in human generation, flesh and spirit work creatively, and bestow on another who is their image, the gift of unending life.

Around the figure of the patriarch and his child then, linger those special circumstances which deepen the worth of this offering in the sight of God. Old age, covenant, promise, first-born, father of believers, hope against hope—in a troubled complicated motet, the theme of divine love is played upon the tortured heart of the father, wounding and healing him.

The father and his son, the "only son," journeyed on together until they reached the place God had shown. Here Abraham built an altar, and set the wood in order on it; then he bound his son Isaac and laid him on the altar, above the pile of wood. He reached out and took up the knife, to slay his son.

It is as though the Crucifixion of Christ were being dramatically mimed in a primitive setting. On one stage, the journey to Calvary; the Heavenly Father, visibly present in the submissive will of the Redeemer. On a lower stage, the passage to the land of Clear Vision, and to the mountain. The father an aged man, the son bearing the wood for sacrifice. The dialogue spontaneous, concentrating on occurrence rather than on human reaction. Abraham is recognized as bearing the Father's will for weapon; "He was led like a lamb to the slaughter, he was led and opened not his mouth" (Isa. 53:7). The holiness of the son holds itself in readiness for death. His love of God has been so pure and strong in life that in death he sees no terror. His equable mind is formed not of Stoic hardness but of the believing courage that dwells habitually within the darkness of mystery. "The Father did not spare His only Son, but gave Him for our sake" (John. 3:16). Christian liturgy approaches the mystery of the Father's will by summoning the great spirit of Abraham, to correct and purify human judgment, to teach Who God is.

Is God love? Yes, for His word has said so (1 John 4:8).

But how can this love be at the same time merciful and without mercy? Because it acts from eternity, and does not hesitate to demand that man's will submit to it by faith.

But is it not intolerable that the same God who offers gifts to men, and is the source of all benefit, should at will snatch these away?

The man of faith finds intolerable only the word *intolerable* itself, when this is applied to God's dealings with men. For man's access to the divine life is not through temporal or even spiritual blessings, considered in themselves, but through union with the Father's will by faith. There is no other access to Him. And one cannot conclude that this access will be won on man's terms. His promise to be "their God" implies the reciprocal bond implied in "They shall be my people." God does not come to man in man's image—as a servant to the human. God is God.

If one were to sum up, then, the meaning of the events at Horeb as they represent an advance in man's religious history, they could be called a new revelation of the transcendance of God.

To know that God is God will cost man bitter suffering. After the Fall, man can no longer simply and gently hold in consciousness these two poles of reality: God is man's friend, and God is the all-holy Omnipotent One. Man can no longer contain the perfect image of things as they are. Or let us rather say that he will preserve himself from false worship only at the cost of suffering.

Only purified man, that is, will be religious man. The pagan heart accepts one or another pole of reality for reality itself, and either creates a god who is in fact merely human, or distorts divine realities into a euphoric and irrelevant dream.

But Abraham represents religious man at a new stage of friendship with God. He is man more deeply conscious of reality. He has accepted suffering into the scheme of his religious life. In the light of Abraham's greatness, then, it becomes clearer that the covenant made with Noe awaited perfection, and awaited it through suffering. The former cosmic covenant had not escaped imperfection, since it had taught the fidelity of God through a rather crude parable of material things—the natural cycles of seasons and days.

But now the covenant moves mysteriously nearer man's spirit, and nearer perfection. In Abraham, man is not merely given one or two generalized laws to test his fidelity. Infinitely more painful, the covenant demands a personal death. The Covenant with God will test man to the heart.

So God's revelations to Abraham set up paradoxes which have nothing in common with human logic. Is there a conflict between the vocation of human fatherhood, and that of son of God? Can love even for one's child suddenly become an obstacle to the love of one's Creator? Without a deep faith from God, the mind of man will inevitably blunder over these queries.

For the point of questions like these is precisely that they probe existence at its roots. They no longer allow reality to be taken for granted by man; neither the reality of God, nor of His gifts. They suddenly lay bare the musculature of man's spirit. They remind man that his natural power of love remains his good servant only as long as no crisis arises. But let love be threatened or challenged, and it will abruptly assert its claims. It lives a separate life after all— it has an organism of its own, it knows pain, it battles against separation or sacrifice. In crisis, love awakens to choices, and the awakening is named suffering; and of all contingencies, suffering is the one for which man is least prepared.

But sacrifice is needful to man. Abraham's sacrifice teaches how deeply true this is. The covenant, after this man has suffered, is no longer hidden in parables or sustained by merely animal sacrifice. In Abraham, the covenant will be transmitted by certain rites performed on the flesh of man. It will bring pain to his infancy, teaching him to weep even before his mind can know the meaning of sorrow. "Every male child of yours will be circumcised" (Gen. 17:10).

Life at its source is consecrated to God. A sign is given to man of the divine predilection. The Israelites will carry upon their flesh the seal of the covenant; it will be a sign that they, as bearers of life, are bearers of the promise also. The two are from now forward interchangeable. The seed of man will issue from his flesh as through a sacred portal, already marked with the sign of the Lord's blessing.

Still we note a paradox. The circumcision places God's seal on the flesh of His chosen people, guaranteeing them a blessing that will outlast time. Yet, in the hour of his testing, Abraham received a command which seemed to turn the promise to nothing. The circumcision and its attendant blessing—what could their value be at all, since the fruit of his loins, the child Isaac, the one on whom all the future depended, was ordained slain? Fruitfulness and sacrifice—how to resolve these two, set against each other like warriors of the Most High, each of them claiming human life for itself, each bearing equal title of origin from God?

They are resolved by the man who walked between them, ignoring their drawn weapons, with the name of God on his his lips—I Am Faithful. When God had first made the covenant with Abraham, He told him to take certain animals and bring them to the divine Presence. "And he brought them to Him, and cut them in half, laying the two halves of each on opposite sides" (Gen. 15:10). And God passed in blazing fire and smoke between the pieces of flesh. He passed there alone, for He alone initiated the covenant which was announced here.

So in the crisis of Isaac's sacrifice, mindful that the God Whose name is Love is unalterable in love, Abraham quietly obeyed. Like a man of stone, he passed through the swords of the dilemma of God; and at his faith, the weapons fell to the ground. They were given that day, as he had been given, a new name. Justice and mercy embraced.

He did not understand at that time something he would later come to understand—something all men would know through him. It was still hidden from him that this hour of sacrifice was the hour when his faith was perfected. His obedience to God was his true circumcision; then the knife fell, not upon his flesh, nor into the body of his son, but into his own will. It fell into his self-will, into the judgment which would presume to say, "I am God's son, but first of all, I am Isaac's father." Abraham had slain the pride which would declare, "I am God's son, yes; but it is a greater thing to be father of a nation than to be son of God. For according to the former I am subject to God, but according to the latter, I shall be like God." No: Abraham "put his faith in God, and it was reckoned virtue in him."

To the sacrifice of Abraham, believers will always turn, to gain the insight which only faith can shed on suffering. The sacrifice, one learns, was interrupted, but in all essentials, it was already completed. For the sacrifice which God demanded was not the death of the son. It was the will of the father—a will brought to filial submission. In obedience, the pride of Abraham had been slain. And God could now greet him as loving son, when the Father Himself, as the "angel of restraining," held the hand of Abraham from the deathblow. "Do not lay hands on the boy, he said, do nothing of the sort to him; for I know now that you revere God, in that you have not withheld your son, your only son, from me" (Gen. 22:12).

The knowledge the believer gains here is like a simultaneous light and darkness. It is an increase of knowledge concerning the dealings of God with man. But this knowledge is in itself darkness. It does not destroy the mystery under which the man of faith lives; it deepens it. As a holy believer Abraham had met his hour of crisis; a patient love had prepared it, and the same love had prepared Abraham's heart for it.

Except for this testing, and its shocking overtones, one might have concluded that the ascent of man to God was a peaceful delight. Abraham, we might have thought, would advance toward God like an aging Adam, with his virtues radiantly upon him, and peaceably enter Eternity.

But God's ways are not man's ways, as God's word imperiously tells us. Who after all can define the perfect man, except the God who knows man's heart? The glance of God derides the definitions man would give to holiness. For man presumes that at a certain arbitrary moment chosen by man, God calls a halt to further purification.

We learn from Abraham's holiness how inaccurate such a notion is. God continued to explore, far into Abraham's old age, the great realities of death, risk, mystery, faith, love, renouncement. And to this same pedagogy, all men are invited. They read in Abraham how the All-Holy deals with the men He has chosen. They come to know that the choice of God is not finished within a moment of time, but is a process which lies upon a man's whole life.

The hour of his suffering and submission was Abraham's greatest hour. Sacrifice from the point of view of faith was accomplished in the heart of the father.

So the Church can honor him as an image of the Fatherhood of God. Perhaps no phrase in the Bible is dearer to the believer's heart than the one God spoke to Abraham: "Take your son, your only son, and sacrifice him to Me." It would seem that the same phrase was in John's mind when he summed up the themes of man's faith and the Father's love, meeting in the sacrifice of Jesus. "God so loved the world as to give his only son . . . that they who believe in Him might not perish, but might have life everlasting" (John 3:16).

3 Imagination and Covenant

The Israelitic covenant moved forward in time under the sign of suffering. Where man had sinned man must atone, as the law made clear. And this law of suffering, as it touched man, refused to remain at a polite distance from him, to be content with his religious gestures. To remark this is to note in Scripture the jealousy of God. Whether the covenant is made with a small obscure tribe, or definitively, with the whole race, God will simply not tolerate an empty religious externalism.

But Jewish history is also a reminder that the gaining of an authentic religious spirit is not the work of a day or an hour. It is a painful process, long-drawn-out and ruled by patience. And the union with God, which is its end, comes to men by way of a death. The individual, the nation, must die to collective and personal guilt before it can presume to say, "We are Your people." Otherwise, as even pagan religious practice admitted, the city shelters a plague in its midst, and risks the destructive hand of the Deity.

Because death is the password to union with God in the period of history that follows the sin of Adam, the race of men advances to God by way of sacrifice. The stench of blood outpoured, the formal gesture, the hieratic rite— all express the urge of men to attain life through death. The race of men, as sacrifice implies, is on its way to a lost identity; and the journey itself is by way of death. In the desert, in sin abounding and hope deferred, in acknowledgment of paganism in its midst, in purification and sin-offering, men are forbidden the luxury of self-forgetfulness, the loss of corporate identity.

And over and above the rite of sacrifice, reinforcing it and probing its integrity, God insists on personal sacrifice. No mere gesture will suffice; man's own heart is demanded. This truth has a universal force. The king will be summoned from his throne, and his bondwoman also. The innocent will suffer, and the guilty by going free will read their own doom; they are not of the noble blood line of God's people. So in Jewish history, the great patriarchs will be chosen along with their sons. Every man must submit to suffering; there is no other way to friendship with God.

To this reality of suffering and its summons, man is commonly tempted to claim exemption, were it not for the fact that the supreme example of the force of the law is a divine one. The mounting of the altar by Isaac, the sacrifice of Abel and of Melchisedec—these are not the high hour of the law of sacrifice in history. They are humanly great, but beside the reality they fade into mere images.

At the great hour of the new covenant, when friendship and love for man have been declared definitively by the lips of God, all men may read in the face of a Man the very expression of love for the Father. It is at this hour that sacrifice will become itself. "I myself will come and save them." The hour has struck. The Lord's public task is done; He sits for a final repast with His brothers.

The law of life through a death, the sealing of covenant, the friendship between God and man: these were the themes to be gathered together by the Lord on this holy night of the final Pasch. The commerce between earth and heaven is resumed, not in Sinaitic visions, but in the guise of a simple community meal—in a Mystery which dwells in the veins of mortal life, and does not disdain to wear its clothing and countenance.

So in Christ, covenant is announced anew. It had survived the centuries, the stain of human contact. Now its hour of supreme fulfillment is come. The divine love is proclaimed, not at a distance, but by the Friend, the meek One Who had entered the Holy City to claim a few friends for His own, to celebrate a religious feast, and to die.

The celebration of the Pasch was at hand. It was a commemoration of the providential deliverance of the people of the old covenant some fifteen hundred years before. And the Lord sat to supper with His Twelve. His face wore the changeful cast which man assumes when his hour sounds— the sorrow of leave-taking, a look of decision, of grief and patience and joy. And from His form and gesture, as a cur-

rent will charge a metal with its power, controlled and con-
trolling, the divinity shone.

The ancient friendship with God, which from man's point
of view had been so faulty, is canceled. It was worn with
desert travel, violated and rent by a history of sin. But even
better than canceled, it is now made new. As childhood is
fulfilled in man, as uncertainties and whims of judgment
are set like a bone structure, firm and supple, strong and
cunningly articulated—so this friendship matures in the new
covenant.

It would perhaps be nearer the truth to say that friendship with God was not so much announced by the Saviour
as simply pointed out once more, by a new Presence. Friendship with God is no longer proclaimed by an intermediary,
a prophet, but by God Himself Who says, "Behold, I come."

We can gain from human dealings an approximation of
the depth of the meaning of the new covenant, as the Saviour's person perfects it. Friendship has the power within
itself, as we know from human life, to set all differences
right, even the differences which have threatened the friendship itself. In the power of its self-renewal, friendship
can nullify a painful history and announce a present of such
worth that whatever had marred its past becomes simply
irrelevant. And this is true also in regard to the covenant of
God and man. Granted, says the Lord's saving action, that
all had not been well with the covenant, that distance between the divine and human had complicated it, that community between God and men had become a duty rather
than a spontaneous joy. All of this was true: but it was
simply of no matter, for the Friend had come.

The sacred word *friend* deepens our understanding of

the covenant. For the Friend is innocent; better, He is innocence itself. And the men He comes to are burdened with the weight of a sin whose power they have almost lost heart to weigh, it has pressed upon them so long and so bitterly. They believe in God to a point, they love Him, but their love seldom rises above a feeling that life must be gotten through somehow; their lives are a kind of no man's land between desperation and virtue. They love, but they have little spontaneity, almost little taste for love.

But now Jesus took the cup after the supper and said, "This cup is the new covenant in my blood, which shall be shed for you. Drink you all of this" (Luke 22:20).

"The new covenant in my blood." The Jews understood, as the Church understands, that there can be no forgiveness without bloodletting. It was a law of mercy which sin had made expedient for man. For without the shedding of blood, man would have no rubric in which to read, as he must read if he is to be saved, the enormity of his offense against Holiness.

But in blood, man can understand the meaning of both sin and forgiveness, which at one period of the covenant had been symbolized by temporal deliverance in Egypt. The blood which the Jews were told to sprinkle on the doorposts had signified the merciful passage of God's anger. So the Twelve who reclined at table with the Lord many hundreds of years later remembered with every ritual gesture the saving act of Jahweh in Egypt on the night of His providence.

When we think of the Twelve Apostles in the period before Pentecost, perhaps we are tempted, in the way of many Christians, to pity them—for childishness, for the petty display of ambition and jealousy with which the Master must often have contended. And yet one must not fail to recognize a common treasure in these men—the recurrent observance of their liturgy, the heritage of Israel. If anything, it was this which gave hope to the Lord as He persevered in their formation. Paganism had left their souls relatively untouched. These men contained, in spite of all the defects of their religious lives, a subconscious wealth of unfructified and vital religious images—such images as the passage of the sea, the desert, the bronze serpent, the promise, the Pasch. Their faith was largely unrationalized, and this was a defect of their simplicity. But at the same time, they had escaped the common defects of the religious spirit of their times—formalism and syncretism.

These twelve men were, for better or for worse, the summit of Israel's religious journeyings toward God. On their behalf the power of God had acted throughout history. For their sake the pagan had been destroyed and his altars leveled. Children of the last Jewish era, these men were formed to the contour of the womb that had borne them to sacred life. Mother Israel, intolerant and favored, recidivist and forgiven, destroyer even of her greatest sons, unpredictable and fitful in good, had borne these men to be the first men of the new covenant.

For the sake of Israel, the nations had laid foundation stones of law, achievements of art and literature, astronomy, medicine, drama. They were to sustain at their very peak a single capstone, Israel, higher than all the other nations by reason of the Hand that had raised and set it there. Israel had become the point of intersection with God, to give everything below her a final shape so that even paganism might, in spite of itself, gesture beyond itself.

The Pasch dramatized Israel's aspirations and history in a sacred rite. The Disciples and the Master gathered to eat the Pasch and to celebrate the Mercy of God in Jewish history. The memories of these men were resonant with a summons to prayer and suffering, a word of exile and return, of sin and forgiveness. The lamb lay upon the table. That afternoon, its blood had been poured out on the temple altar. Now in the guise of a banquet they were to make live again the dramatic story of God's love for His people.

Each of the Disciples on that night was like a man who says, "I am in love." And so he knows at any great moment of his life that he is himself because of that love; it has made him man. And even if such a man be thoughtless and crude, there is hope for him because love hopes on, and creates while it hopes. So it was with the friends of the Lord. Their history had formed them to this night. The love of God had created them for the sake of this night. That love now immersed them in an action which summoned their holy past and gave instinctive homage to the unmeasured mystery of life.

They had been formed to this night. A tide of history moved them toward it. The lamb before them now, the bitter herbs, the cup passing among them, hallel and blessing— all their holy past was present to them. It was Israel's anamnesis.

As men at any point of history, they were aware fully of their past; but they were unaware that they were being formed to a future. They sang of God's mercies, but they knew nothing of the mercies that awaited them in the event this night would celebrate. They could not know that their descendants would sing of an even greater mercy than their fathers had known. The Christian liturgy of this same night would sing of it;

> This is the Paschal feast, in which the true Lamb is slain, whose blood hallowed the doorposts of the faithful. This is the night on which You brought our forefathers from Egypt, dryshod through the Red Sea. It is of this night that Scripture says, "And the night shall be bright as the day, and the night shall light up my joy."

The memories of the Apostles were enriched by the rite they shared. If it is true to say that they were primitive men, the term is the very opposite of denigration. Without attempting to idealize them out of all reality, it still remains true that their imaginations were largely unweakened by loss of conviction, by the shift of truth into mere fashion. Their cast of mind was largely imaginative; it was hardly discursive at all. It was nourished by religious image and type, and grew in this atmosphere. And their imaginations had been formed by centuries of a religious tradition, vivid, sanguinary, harshly drawn, immensely powerful—the echoes of prophetic word and witness, of community sacrifice renewed, and renewed again.

In order to realize the impact which religious history had had upon the imaginations of the Disciples, we might turn to the twelfth chapter of the Book of Exodus. It recounts the story of the night of the deliverance of God's people from Egypt. Having sacrificed the lamb and eaten it, standing with clothing girt about them, and having painted the doorposts with the blood of the lamb as their sign of protection, the Israelites departed. It was a sorrowful journey, but one radiant with the word of the covenant. The Exodus had begun.

The people had consumed the lamb. And this symbol of innocence and suffering would be summoned again and again into the consciousness of the believing Jew. On the night of deliverance, the blood of the lamb had assured the people of deliverance and its body had been their nourishment. And at the dawn of the new covenant, the Lamb of God would be hailed on His appearance at the Jordan. And finally, at the end of things, the vision described by St. John speaks of the same image: "I saw a Lamb, as it were slain, but victorious" (Apoc. 5:6).

This sacred history had lived on in the Jews and had become viable in the Disciples of Jesus, at length. And it was a matter not merely of codes and rites, but of the living imagination of man.

By impregnating the imagination this living image, constantly renewed, enriched, modified by history and by encounter with the present, meets the religious needs of man at every age and renews him through the imagination. The Jews of any period of their own history could discover that the image of the Lamb, had, in a true sense, gone before them. It was older than themselves, it gathered up their religious history, the divine graces which had sustained men. So the image contained and invited them to the mystery of their fathers' meeting with God.

And for the Christian the same symbol is operative, with the difference that it has become a divine one, the Lamb of

God. And the image, it must be insisted, is still strictly historical. It gathers up its Jewish history and baptizes it. And because the Christian image of the Lamb has unfolded historically and is not presented merely as a datum and imposed on man, it teaches man gradually and with infinite gentleness the nature of Christian reality. It opens before him the fulfillment of Christian life by way of suffering, the Christian altruism which may even demand the gift of one's life for the sake of the other.

The image is at once substantial and spiritual, holy and familiar, imbedded in the past and yet renewed on the altar of each day. So by its complex richness, it constantly invites man to go out of himself into the infinite, and to return to himself in the finite. In this way, too, man is kept open before divine and human reality, neither condemned to the merely human nor deceived in Promethean daydreams.

In understanding the crucial place which the imagination occupies in the religious life, even primitive paganism was true to man in a way men today have almost forgotten. Paganism dealt deliberately in images, as a matter of the substance of the religious life. And by this tactic it could affect human motive deeply and continually because, in however crude and imperfect a way, it drew upon man's unawakened powers of prayer and action.

The flaw with the pagan images was that they had no spiritual counterparts. They quite literally stood for nothing; they were human fabrications. They were often of great dignity and nobility, but they were images of man even though they were named and venerated as God. The pagan image-making was a process of ventriloquism; ironic and even tragic, since the image was no better than a carved doll amplifying man's voice, reacting to his thought and word, dressed in his weakness and vices, and named *god*.

This pagan image had no power of divinizing man. It had the vicious power, on the other hand, of convincing man, in the name of religion, that the divine was no more than an extension of the human; that the divine merely enlarged human good, or human happiness, or human sins. But the image denied in principle any scission between the two orders of being, divine and human. So the pagan imagination formed by these images had no power of stretching man's grasp toward a synthesis. In place of spiritual enlargement, the best it could offer the believer was the fantastic; a voyage that pretended to leap free from the gravity of this world by striking straight off into the infinite—without concept, without history, without the body, without imagination.

The Jewish and Christian image of the Lamb is of a different value entirely. It had the power of forming the imagination of the people of God. And it did this by allowing to crystallize around it the sacred accretions of God's commerce with man, and of man's response. Such images as deliverance, mercy, forgiveness, outpouring of blood, innocence slain on behalf of man—all these gathered about the central image of the Lamb. In this way it led man imperceptibly and simply and gently in the direction of God. This image was the lowly approximation, fitted to man's nature, of God's altruism, of His love at the service of man's need. At the same time, the path by which the Image led man was no projection away from the earth and time and the exigency of the present. The Image spoke the language of man's present, and did this in an imaginative way. By the assimilation of the flesh of the lamb, and by the sprinkling of its blood, man was invited to growth in those spiritual qualities for which the Lamb literally stood—sacrifice and innocence. In such a way the Image refused man the luxury of exemption from the community need, and from his own obligation to worship God.

By setting up these poles, infinite-finite, transcendant-vulnerable, the Image of the Lamb continued to keep man open to God, and to keep him himself. The Image avoided the illusions of paganism that would persuade man that the way to the divine must strike free from the material world, thus burying him in the fantastic in the name of spiritual liberation.

So the Lamb image accompanied man through the centuries of Jewish and Christian religious history. It was an image of the earth, and an image of eternity. It was born in time, submitted to death at the hands of men, invited them to partake of itself as nourishment at their spiritual banquet, and finally it arose again, the Image of immortality: "I saw a lamb, slain and yet victorious."

Summoning all the experiences of man's life to itself, undergoing them in its own flesh; subject to the human cycles of death, yet so far superior to death as to rupture its power; at the service of the needs of man, yet their leader and king; giving of its flesh and blood, yet never diminished or divided; placing burdens on man's faith and trust, yet in the act of giving itself, nourishing that same faith and hope; summoning man to death and victory, not as mere charades for contemplation, but as calls to action and suffering—so would run a few of the infinitely various adumbrations of the Image of the Lamb.

And this Image, it must be understood, is a dramatic one. It is not a mere static datum of the imagination; rather, it aims by action and crisis to lead man in its own direction. It sets up an ideal of grandeur that will lead humanity beyond time; its goal is eternity.

And yet in this process it invites man to become more intensely human precisely in accepting the experience of the divine. It would make him more fit for the task of the present, because in welcoming the divine summons, man is freed from the slavery of his present. It beckons man out of himself into its own sacred content, and this not by way of escape, but by an ecstasy that renews and heals time itself. The Image intensifies man's link with his brothers, finally, not as a juridical or conceptual pact, but as a choice in love, sealed with blood in the midst of a banquet of friendship and unity.

Possibility and actuality are two great poles of this Image. The Image is actual, as concretized and *here,* as verifiable in history. It opens man's potential before him, in the shocking and dramatic evidence of what a Man has done for men. So the Image offers men a horizon of love which is literally without limit, because it is divine. But also because this Image is divine it can encompass and integrate the human. It reminds man that his love is forbidden the refuges of vague formulas, of remaining historically uncorrected and unpurified. The Image gathers into unity all the events that are of eternal relevance to man. It tells man what is possible to him by reminding him of what has been actual to One in his midst. So man's inner possibility is kept from illusion through the history of the Lamb—deliverance of men at the price of one's own death, and victory as the reward of heroic altruism. And this is the master cycle, not only of the Lamb, as though He were apart or inviolate or finished with, but of the believer also.

Man's love of God is thus given form, containment, and direction. The Image of the Lamb does not allow man or his love to rest in concept or empyrean self-approval. It rather summons his love to a task, a task which is identical with the task of the Image itself. The Lamb gently reminds man that Christian love is not free, in the sense that it can seek fulfillment in mere caprice or in mere promises.

But the gift of this Image is precisely that it forms man to the Christian vocation. It gives to the pure possibility of man a direction, a thing to be done, a living example, a call to fidelity and dedication.

Through the Image, what is possible to man moves imperceptibly into the realm of the probable, and thence to the actual. The actual, of course, cannot be a first stage of man's life, if this actuality is to be equivalent to his full spiritual stature. Man must rather pass through the bewildering area where all things are possible, where one must call for help in order to choose, where choice itself is terrifyingly unfamiliar.

Man must be forced to ask questions, if his answers are to have any meaning. What to do? Or perhaps, to do nothing? At this stage of possibility, even the idea of no choice at all had a fatal attraction for man. Christianity has not yet assumed such force within his heart that the consequences of not choosing are clearly seen. And to remain at that stage of things, not to abandon the warmth and security of non-choice—this is the first temptation of all.

One must be ejected into birth by a summons of God, a

mercy which calls an end to the period of spiritual gestation. Man has come from no choice at all, to an infinite possibility of choices. His imagination is still pagan, in the sense that it is not yet submitted; it ranges above religion and nature, and finds no reason to choose. Or perhaps it goes through the gesture of having submitted to the Christian Image; it acts as though it had chosen rightly, and may even indulge in this play-acting in all sincerity, because it sees the advantages of faith, of welcoming the truth as truth. But it cannot choose as yet; the image has not yet grown upon the imagination to a point where it will permeate all of man. Faith and Christianity are, so far, only probable.

But by a grace which is both gift and choice, faith becomes actual. Man is now contained within the sacred Image; he is brought to it, he has entered within it, he has been shaped and nourished by it. Christianity knows its victory. What had been merely possible to man, became slightly more present to him by way of probability, and then finally was actualized. And as the least probable thing in nature is that a man should exist at all, so the least probable thing in the order of grace is that there should be a single Christian. In both cases God delights to show first of all the purely possible, and then to finitize it in the actual.

And this process is named, in two senses, creation, as Saint Paul tells us. The least probable thing in the order of nature is that there should be this man, a man of imagination, open to possibility, yet himself actual and physical and present. And the least probable thing in the order of grace is that there should be this Christian, his love given its form and history and actuality by the summons of God.

His imagination defines the Christian, and it frees him.

It gives him actuality in many ways. He is actually son of God, brother to all men, heir of the Kingdom of God. Yet none of those ways, nor their sum which we named the Paschal mystery, reduces a man's freedom, or diminishes his personality. This man remains, in a very true sense, a pure possibility, untouched in his freedom, with his own way to go, and his own pace to set, by his own choice. The Image is only a beckoning, an invitation of sweetness and strength. It no more forces man or is capable of forcing him, than is the lamb of nature. The destiny which the Image opens and invites man to, can be refused. The events It once submitted to and now reigns over can be denied by man, as far as their relevance to his life are concerned. The consent which the Image invokes can be refused or pre-empted or taken back. The spaces of man's life which the Image fills with light and healing and grace and courage can be emptied again, and a pagan vacuum restored—the void of the merely possible, or the chaos of non-choice. All that had been united in this Image can be dissociated once more.

The adult Christian remains free. And this freedom has its degrees of strength. One might almost say that in a given Christian, the force of actual freedom is in ratio to the force with which he met and welcomed his own possibility. If the image of his faith has imaginative density and stability, it is because he brought these qualities to his new life at its very inception. If on the other hand he is mediocre and unconvinced, the fault cannot be with the grace which has formed him. The fault lies rather around some human failure. The actuality of Christian life had been created too hastily, or welcomed without preparation or thought, or merely constructed out of the example of others or of idealism or of rhetoric. Probably one would be right in saying that grace had formed no true image at all, because human defects had prevented it.

We often have cause to mourn, in ourselves or in others, the minimal Christian life which man gives evidence of. At times even a public and scandalous failure will occur. Believers are shocked, the weak are scandalized. It seems as though a great work had been inexplicably destroyed overnight. If we look for a solution to these mysterious setbacks, Scripture suggests at least one line of thought that may be of help. God himself has reminded us in dealing with His people that the processes of time are essential to human formation. And this remains true when the invitation to grace is in question. It was not by divine caprice that the Jewish people were led so long and so far, until the promised One came to them. Had He come suddenly, the event would have been consonant with God's perfection, but it would have left man sorely unprepared. For the Incarnation truly to win men to God, centuries of patient preparation were required—men must be born and live and die in hope of a promise. During whole generations evil was not forcibly suppressed by God—it was tolerated in patience. God allowed the nation to sin, to expiate and to return to him. Century after century taught men the meaning of the divine mercy.

It is the same with the Christian. No believer attains his vocation in Christ who has not first experienced the history of God's saving action within himself. These saving actions we name the Sacraments of Christ. They sum up not only man's contact with the flesh of the Lamb here and now—they allow this man to enter really and deeply into the history of God's salvation. They permeate man with a sense of sacred history, a history which has at length willed to include him. And they require as a consequence, in order to do their great work well, that man give them time and attention.

So the Incarnation is the final word of God on His attitude toward time. In the Image of the Lamb, now identified with God Himself, God becomes subject to change and to growth. His life among man will not hesitate in a sense to subject God to an historical method, to cause Him to "prove Himself."

Now this same divine attitude toward time, dramatized in the Image of the Lamb, continues in the Church. The believer cannot fail to be deeply moved when he considers how the Image continues to make man's history its own.

The Christians' varied biography has become in a measure the biography of the Lamb. This divine Image works with man, and with man's subjection to time. The laws of human existence, which decree that no living reality springs fully grown from the earth, are taken for Its own. So the Image rejects any tinge of pagan supernature, the brusque and overmastering will to have done with the human, with vulnerability and growth, the will to achieve everything in an hour, to bewilder man with the epiphany of superman.

No, the sacred Image consents to reveal Itself in stages. In this way, the growth of the Image in the imagination of the whole race becomes a parable of the growth of the Image in each man.

That is, the race of man was first only possibly itself, only possibly Christian, in the era of paganism. Then in Judaism the human race became probably Christian. And the case is paralleled in the individual in any period of history. He is first of all only possibly Christian, then probably so, then only finally truly Christian. The Image thus enters into man's religious consciousness gradually and gently, lest he be overwhelmed by an event for which he has undergone no preparation of heart.

And in Christianity a slow unfolding must take place within each man, of the full implications of the Lamb Image. He first learns of the Image as one of nourishment and deliverance, then after a time as a blood offering which will demand of him also the "daily death" of which Paul speaks. Finally the believer will recognize the Image of the Lamb as sign and substance of his own victory:

> Then I saw standing in front of the throne and in the midst of the four beings and of the others, a Lamb as if slain. . . . In my vision I heard a chorus of many angels and of the living beings and elders who encircled the throne. Their number was myriads on myriads and thousands on thousands . . . In a loud voice they said, "Worthy is the Lamb who has been slain to receive power and wealth and wisdom and strength and honor and glory and blessing." . . . The four living beings said, "may it be so." But the elders prostrated themselves and worshipped Him who lives forever and ever.
>
> (Apoc. 5:6-14)

So the Christian is relieved, by the slow assimilation to himself of the Image of the Lamb, of an actuality that would be either fantastic or mechanistic, that had bypassed the possible and never undergone the anguish of the merely probable, and so had arrived at an actuality that was without content or depth. Actuality of this type is almost entirely devoid of imagination. It comes to religious conviction not by way of suffering or personal choice, but by a heavy-handed will to create an actuality for itself out of prejudice or self-will or Philistinism.

Such a Christianity as this has at heart two qualities that Christianity has always rejected—moralism and abstractness.

This pseudo-Christianity cannot accept the consequences of the central announcement of sacred history: "The Word was made flesh and dwelt among us." It could perhaps bear that God should be God; but it cannot in any real sense accept that God should become man. It cannot accept His Manhood as a principle of divine activity in the sense of which Peter Chrysologous wrote: "In human actions, Christ works divine mysteries."

It is of course true that the Incarnation summons man to a new evaluation of his human life. A wary distance from God, a blindness to His presence in the events of human life, a mind that restricts the areas in which the divine is at work and sees in creation only danger and ambiguity, a distrust of the shape which history takes, as though things lay under the curse of God—these are some of the psychic consequences of a faith which has refused fully to accept the Incarnation.

Such a crippled faith cannot imagine, in the sense we have spoken of, that a human body could save, could alter human life from within, or could perform actions of such worth that they brought all mankind to a "leap in being." It could not accept the flesh as an instrument of glory, as a power which at once brings about the new creation, and leads all things toward it. How, it asks, could the human presume to set itself such a height when the Kingdom of

Heaven itself is a final vindication of the spiritual, the free-ing of man from material cosmos which had been a kind of temporary punishment and from which God's will would finally free man?

When such a Christian encounters the works of God in Christ, he is inclined to see them as closed historical com-partments. He knows that they were truly performed within our history, but he comes to conclude that history has also sealed them off. These acts are done with. The Saviour died and rose again, such reasoning admits, and we shall die and rise again. But between these two events, the Saviour's glory and our own, human life goes on, more or less according to a pattern of things set up in the Old Testament.

God is at a distance from man, the law is supreme over the spirit of the law, the flesh of man is the instrument of death. The gift of eternity has already been granted man by the Passion, the Resurrection and the expected return of the Lord; but the time between is nothing. If man is already accepted into eternal life, it is only man's relation to eter-nity which has been altered. Toward time and this world, he is still a stranger or an active enemy. And has not God himself implied the rightness of this attitude on the part of Christians and stamped it with approval in permitting un-believing men, with a frightening unanimity, to reject His name and to turn from the sign in man's midst, His Church?

This view of life insists in effect that a given reality can only be grasped if it is isolated and seen in itself, without relation to other experiences or hierarchies of reality. So a man reasons that time is nothing because he contrasts time to eternity, that the world is nothing because he contrasts the world to the Church, that human striving is nothing because he isolates human striving from eternity. So all the answers which such a method reaches are true, but they are answers to a problem which has been falsely stated.

For the Incarnation of God has welcomed man into the life of God. And we cannot forget that this central event was performed within the envelope of our universe. By an implication as sublime as it is obscure, the Incarnation has not scorned to elevate things human to the dignity of divine instruments. And this dignifying of the human has extended outward from the humiliated flesh of the Saviour, upon which the approval of God rested to the incalculable degree of uniting it to the Godhead. From Christ this approval of God has gone gently outward into the universe, blessing all things as in the days of Genesis; finding all things good.

And as the flesh of man has its master image in the flesh of the Saviour, in which man can read his dignity and his destiny, so analogously with time. A moment of time was sanctified by the choice of the Father, which brought the Word Incarnate to a death of sacrificial and obedient love. From the moment of this choice, the graces of His death and victory sanctify the time that remains to man until the last day. The Lamb of God at a chosen moment saved us. And this moment was so sacred that God claimed it for His own; He called it "My hour." It was the moment when the divine freedom vindicated itself in time. And in choosing time to be the instrument of the vocation of His Son God has in effect chosen all time. He would leave no hour to issue unsanctified from this, "My hour."

So His death and victory has its anamnesis, its effective making-present. God's saving action continues to be an-

nounced from the altars of the believing community; the
Lamb is slain yet glorious. And the things of this world
which were taken in hand by the enemies of God to effect
Christ's death, but which instead of serving human malice
have served divine love, these still lie within the radiance
of the divine irony—a death which was a victory. In a Man,
all these things will see God. As they have served His death,
they will serve His victory.

And even apart from its highest destiny, declared at the
altar, material creation serves man's destiny by not refusing
to serve his present. It continues true to man by serving
"whatever is true, whatever honorable, whatever just, whatever pure, whatever lovable, whatever merits praise"
(Phil. 4:8).

The meaning of this plan of God was suddenly and un-
predictably revealed in a few hours of the Agony of the Son
of God. But this showing forth of the meaning of human
life was not meant to be buried in history. It was master
image of a scheme of things that would endure until the
last day. The visible universe continues to serve that Body
which is upbuilding itself, bone and marrow and organs,
until it has attained the completeness of "Him Who is always and everywhere complete." And it can be said that the
Christian who remains at enmity or a deliberate distance
from this plan of God, declared in the flesh of His Son and
in His Church, cannot have spoken his full *credo* to Christianity.

And it is strange how, once the Incarnation has become
uncomfortable to a believer, he will tend to seek refuge in
an Old Testament spirit that is, from the point of view of
history, infantile. This Christian will regress into the

company of those who once refused to move forward to the consummation of history. So his spirit will be found more and more in sympathy with those who lived when the consciousness of the old covenant was at lowest ebb. There the prophets are silent, religious events are externalized into gesture.

The Christian sensibility we speak of will tend to fit all reality to its own measure. It will be marked by an impatience with depth. It will become more and more doubtful of what is possible to man. It will instinctively transfer to religious life the lifeless images that occur to it from the worlds of commerce, law and the inorganic world. It will demand an abstract and verbal exactness of realities which are necessarily undetermined and of mysterious depth. Finally, it will substitute letter for spirit, and will summon other Christians to answer to its own scientific "judgment."

So, in protest against the imaginative life of religious man, such Christians remain strangers to the attitudes which stream from the Christian imagination itself, and which we name the *Christian mind*. Because such believers have no need of recourse to an image of God, they cannot imagine what it is to fear or to hope or to adore. Their imagination has been pre-empted and possessed by their will; not the will to believe or to submit, to which the Image of the Lamb of God invites man, but the will to dominate, to be central, to "possess" God.

And we note finally in such religious lives a regression to the fatalism and determinism which in the Book of Genesis surround the scene of man's fall. It is as though a single choice had undone all of sacred history, as it was meant to focus and reach its point of concentration on Christian life. The Lamb of God is silent, and at distance. He had corrected the existence of men by the radiance of His sacrificial love; but these gifts can only enter man at man's own welcome. Being refused, they leave the heart a void—without history, or hope, or love of man.

4 Prophecy and Society

The connnection between the covenant and the Israelitic prophets is a necessary one; in fact the appearance of prophets in Israel is a sign that God's will would have the covenant endure. Jewish history is thus a reminder that a man of faith must periodically appear on the human scene —a man whose courageous speech will give substance to law, and correct man's natural tendency toward irreligion and idolatry.

Such tendencies of course are at work among men in all circumstances of life. It would be perhaps unrealistic to come to such a view of man that we consider him easily drawn to worship God in truth. The fact is that the conscience of man is burdened in a hundred ways, all of them conspiring against genuine religious life. Man is victim of pride and lust and the accumulated falsehoods of his history. Unless God intervenes he accepts the lies of his fathers, and lives by them, and passes them on to his sons. And within any given lifetime man's vicious tendencies are active in all circumstances. He is drawn away from the truth by prosperity as well as by sorrow and temporal loss. Against all these enemies there is literally nothing in life that can favor his eternal destiny, except the mercy of God.

Such a view of life must seem overly pessimistic unless we had at hand the accounts of St. Paul of the religious life of his times. In his letter to the Romans, he had spoken in effect of a society cut off from the mercy of God, given over to divine anger. We will perhaps be in a better position to understand the mercy of God toward Israel if we compare her religious life with that of Rome at the same period. The vast difference between the two peoples is in no sense a tribute to the integrity of Israel, considered merely in herself. It is a tribute rather to the mercy which called and created her, "My people"—and having summoned, did not cease to show mercy.

One of the vehicles of that mercy was the continuing line of Jewish prophets.

Their place in the history of Israel is an enormously complex one. These men had bearing on every facet of life—on priesthood and temporal rule, on the laws governing civil life and the sanctuary. But of main interest to us will be the fact that the prophets stood at the forefront of the history of the people of God, and communicated a sacred content to that history.

These men stood firm, first of all, against the many forms of paganism that threatened the people. Their work in this regard was literally never finished with. In the desert of Canaan, the sufferings of the Exodus had brought on murmurings, an indication of weakened faith in God. In the later period of the Kings, material blessings threatened the believers once more—this time with Gentile paganism. Again God's prophets must speak out vigorously and constantly.

Apart from the prophets, then, we are justified in concluding that there is simply no explanation for the integrity and the continuity of religious life in Israel.

And it is not merely a question here of the attrition of time against a given religious tradition, or the way in which even the most fervent beliefs tend to lose force as a society grows older. The plain fact is that Israel was guilty of the same sins for which the pagan nations around her had perished. She was guilty of false worship, of usury, of oppression of the poor, of faithlessness to God in every form. Yet as a matter of history, she never entirely fell away.

What, then, preserved her as herself? Where did she gain courage for the great return, the spirit of amendment which is one of the infallible signs that a religious life remains vital? By any natural standard, she should have perished on any one of a number of occasions; in Egypt, in the desert, in Babylon, during the prosperity of the Davidic era. We are forced to conclude that the pressures of paganism and faithlessness would have drawn her into ruin, without some special and constant evidence of God's love in her midst. And this evidence we name *prophecy*.

In the minds of many Christians the task of prophecy is reduced to a mere foretelling of the future. Throughout Jewish history, however, this is a minor aspect of the prophetic role. We are to think rather of a mediatory task, in which a man is chosen by God and works under His blessing, in order to communicate the divine will to men.

The prophet brings into time, into its vacillations and compromises, the gaze of God, and he judges. And he bears back to God, from his elevated holiness, a report of the state of things among men. Not that God does not already know all things, but He asks mysteriously that the prophet take on himself the burden of solidarity and communication on behalf of men. So the prophet's sense of being a man of divine choice paradoxically embeds him more deeply in the fate of his fellow men.

The prophet could perhaps be best defined as a man of love. He loves men in an altogether extraordinary way; and this love of his abides, even though his vocation excludes the possibility of a normal life among men. The prophet is sent to men almost as a stranger. He is sometimes reverenced, sometimes despised and feared—but never is he in a familial sense one among his brethren.

And yet at their civilized periods, when men are most worthy of the name *man,* they will turn to their prophet in order to learn who they are. Strange and other-worldly, of an abrupt crude impatience even with man's good works, of disturbing queries, of a speech that already inhabits eternity—if men cannot love the prophet, they must admit that he has loved them. He is perhaps the only man who could be called their benefactor.

For without the prophet the oracles are silent, and man becomes involved in a tragic vicious circle of temporal purpose and death. Without prophecy the alliance with God becomes a mere museum piece. It is put aside as the relic of a more credulous past. It becomes simply irrelevant to the decisions of life. Those decisions, taken arbitrarily or under the stress of passion, allow men to be born and to live and to die without knowing the reason for existence.

This situation is illustrated by the later periods of pagan cultures which surrounded Israel. Without prophets speaking in their midst and therefore without access to God, pagan man came to a great acedia with life. He lived on, and envied the dead. He fell into a destructive romanticism, filled with disgust toward a world which contained so much evil, so much defeated purpose and accumulated wrongdoing.

This burden of pessimism lay heavily on the tragic drama of the Greeks, making their genius into a single mourning voice for the sorrow of life. If God is good, they asked again and again, how could things go so ill with man? And if things go so badly, why does man exist at all?

The Jewish prophets stood firmly against this tendency. In contrast with pagan hatred of this world, they insisted that man's source and destiny were determined by the goodness of God. God was Creator of the physical universe, and of man, and both are good. This truth, calmly repeated in the face of all circumstance, of prosperity and the paralysis of luxury, saved man from the corrosion of pagan despair. God is goodness itself, and His creation is the evidence of His goodness. In Hebrew prophecy, this theme sometimes occasions an outburst of sacred poetry, in which the material face of things seems to dissolve before the beauty of One Whose image is everywhere in this world.

The prophets insisted also that a dishonor was offered God if the religious sense of the people moved in the direction of hatred of the world. The theme is a constant of the

Old Testament teaching—so far from being evil, the material universe which gently supports man's life is a parable of the presence of God among men.

In the midst of pagan history, the grave and measured voice of the Israelitic prophet was heard. It insisted on the goodness of God, manifested in history. And this goodness, the prophets taught, did not hesitate to test man. It sometimes destined him to suffering, but to a suffering which was destined to serve man's good. It saved man, if it was properly understood, from the specious victory offered him by this world; it kept him open to God, and to his own destiny.

In Isaias, this theme of human sorrow and its meaning reaches its greatest heights. The book represents perhaps the only point in the Old Testament where the theme of man's suffering approaches the simple grandeur which will surround the death of the Saviour. In the suffering servant, Isaias lifts the curtain of the Holy of Holies for a space, and believing man may see, written in the flesh of the Holy One, the meaning of suffering—the meaning of Christ's suffering, and of his own. The meaning is expiation and a way to glory. If the Father chastises, He does so with a hand of love. And God's love is so exalted and mysterious that it will not hesitate to give the only begotten Son. In the suffering of this Israelite spoken of by Isaias, men may gain new insight into the meaning of innocent expiation, and into the enigma of human suffering in history:

The world stands gazing in horror; was ever a human form so mishandled, human beauty so defaced? Yet this is He who will purify a multitude of nations; kings shall stand dumb in His presence; seen, now, where men had no tidings

of Him, made known to such as never heard His name . . .
No stateliness here, no beauty as we gaze upon Him to win
our hearts. Nay, here is one despised, left out of all human
reckoning; bowed with misery, and no stranger to weakness; how should we recognize that face? How should we
take any account of Him, a man so despised? Our weakness,
and it was He who carried the weight of it, our miseries,
and it was He who bore them. A leper, so we thought of
Him, a man God had smitten and brought low; and all the
while it was for our sins he was wounded, it was guilt of
ours crushed Him down; on Him the punishment fell that
brought us peace, by His bruises we were healed. Strayed
sheep all of us, each following his own path; and God laid
on His shoulders our guilt, the guilt of us all.

(Isa. 52, 53)

In the case of Jeremiah, suffering is not so much the
theme of a man's writing as the theme of life itself. This
great spirit, conscious of weakness and even of personal
revolt against the call of God, nonetheless arose to the
grandeur of his prophetic vocation. He had been timid and
without recourse either to powerful friends, or to an in-
herently strong view of life and its demands. He felt himself abandoned and subjected to an overwhelming sense of
incapacity. But God chose him. He filled this empty vessel
with His Spirit.

The word of the Lord came to me, and His message was;
I claimed thee for my own before ever I fashioned thee in
thy mother's womb. Before ever thou camest to the birth,
I set thee apart for myself. I have a prophet's errand for thee
among nations. Alas, alas, Lord God, said I, I am but a
child that has never learned to speak. A child, sayst thou?
the Lord answered. Nay, I have a mission for thee to under-

take, a message to entrust to thee. Have no human fears;
am I not at thy side, to protect thee from harm? the Lord
said. And with that, the Lord put out his hand, and
touched me on the mouth; see, He told me, I have inspired
thy lips with utterance. Herein now I give thee authority
over the nations; with a word thou shalt root them up and
pull them down, overthrow and lay them in ruins; with
a word thou shalt build them up and plant them anew.

(Jer. 1:4-10)

In general, the earlier prophets had stressed the communal aspects of punitive suffering. It became a Hebrew commonplace that the sins of the fathers were visited upon the
sons. But Ezechiel proved himself boldly original in thought.
Instead of stressing the social nature of sin and revolt, he
became the architect of a new individualism. A celebrated
vision, recounted in Chapters VIII to XI of his book, gave
him his point of departure. From this vision, and from the
rigorous application of its principles, he went on to score
the madness of the men whose choices set themselves against
the just God. Ezechiel even leads man to the eventual realization of a divine justice which leads beyond the grave, with
justice and love reconciled. The final word on suffering,
he implies, cannot be said within time.

As far as human life was concerned, Ezechiel had no good
news for men. He lived in a time of great national suffering;
entering the fate of his people with sublime courage, he
loosed from the depths a cry of such power and grace that
men still draw hope from it. In Ezechiel we note how history
has become the instrument of God's providence, and of its
announcement to man. This prophet, as man of that providence, during his whole lifetime refused to accept or to

give a false comfort. He refused, on the one hand, to announce a conversion of the people when none had in truth occurred. And he refused to announce falsely that the justice of God was satisfied with men as they were—selfish, half-hearted, deeply aligned with the forces of this world.

The sins of his community fired him with a passionate zeal for God's honor. Seeing the divine honor outraged, he awaited like a tragic protagonist the vindication of the justice of God in the destruction of human hope. It was only, Ezechiel said, when man had been reduced to a heap of dry bones, that God could make of him a new creation.

> The Lord's power laid hold of me, and by the spirit of the Lord I was carried away and set down in the midst of a plain, which was covered with bones. Round the whole extent of them He took me, heaped up high on the plain, and all of them parched quite dry. Son of man, He said, can life return to these bones? Lord God, said I, Thou knowst. Then He bade me utter a prophecy over the bones; listen, dry bones, to the word of the Lord. A message to these bones from the Lord; I mean to send my spirit into you, and restore you to life. Sinews shall be given you, flesh shall grow on you, and skin cover you; and I will give you breath to bring you to life again; will you doubt the Lord's power?
>
> (Ezek. 37:1-6)

We learn from Ezechiel the depths of the plan of God with regard to man's life, even when this holy will must encounter and deal with human malice. The prophets' symbols and parables insist on one great theme—man will reach the will of God only by a lifelong purification, inviting him more deeply into the mystery of his redemption.

The theme of personal suffering, so vividly present to the major prophets, has always been understood by the Church in a double sense. The prophets truly and historically suffered; they were innocent, and the wicked put them to the test. But there is more to their greatness than this. They were able to speak and suffer and die as an image of Someone else—One Whom history awaited—Someone, we might add, of whose coming they probably were unaware, since their writing was invariably focused on the just kings whom the Davidic line was to produce.

Still, from the vantage point of the Incarnation, Christian believers may learn from the prophets how astonishingly the historical Christ surpassed all the accumulated hopes of man's religious history.

As far as the individual prophet is concerned, we are under no burden of believing that he was conscious of speaking for Christ. The account of the suffering servant in Isaiah is a good case in point here. Was the author writing of himself, or of Israel, or of some contemporary Jew who had undergone unjust suffering and death? Or was he perhaps granted a revelation of the sufferings of Christ? The question is a vexing one. But we might venture to answer that he was quite possibly speaking of all of these. And our answer would remain valid even though the writer was conscious, at the time he wrote, of only one or another of the possibilities we have mentioned. We are in no position, from the point of view of historical knowledge, of giving a final answer. And even if we were, and the field of possibility were to be narrowed down to one man, it is true that the author of Isaiah would in a large sense have illuminated the sufferings and death of Christ, and their mystery.

For the prophet is not the sole author of his account. We believe that in a mysterious way the Holy Spirit led him into depths of which he may have had no, or very little, notion. So we are free, for very good reasons, in concluding that the human author was guided supernaturally to include in his words a wider meaning than he may have been conscious of.

Our reasons for this conclusion would be mainly two. The first and most important is that on given occasions Our Lord Himself told us that such and such a statement from the Old Testament had reference to Him. So He would borrow a phrase and declare that beyond any doubt it was true of Him. Even "borrowed" is a poor word here; what He often did was to claim certain statements of the prophets as His own, in somewhat the same manner as an owner will claim his possessions. It was almost like the case of a man legally vindicating his own name against interlopers or false claimants, or against the thoughtlessness of men and the inaccuracies that tend to accumulate in history. (This illustration will be of help, especially if we recall that most of the Jewish names were not arbitrary constructions, but referred to a precise function.) So when Our Lord died, He chose to die with phrases of Psalm Twenty-one on His lips. In this way, He was claiming for Himself the name of Jesus, which was also a title. It meant the One who saves. And the good Jew who cared to know who Christ was could recall from the triumphant ending of the Psalm that the promised One was here and now saving His people, in circumstances that were dramatizing the ancient words exactly.

Our second guide as to the prophetic words of a given passage of the Old Testament is, of course, the Church herself. Her declarations on this point are remarkably few.

But in spite of her silence, the Church is rather constantly insisting on the prophetic content of the Old Testament authors. And to the one who truly understands her this will not appear arbitrary or forced.

Her liturgy is instructive in this regard. When for example the Introit of a given Mass borrows a few phrases from a Psalm, and refers them to Our Lord, the Church is not claiming a literal prophecy. She is declaring what we might call the radical fittingness that underlies human life, especially when life's great themes come to mind—themes like sacrifice, love for others, exaltation of heart, the failures of man against God's love. It is not at all strange then that the prophets, who were men of acutely human sensitivity, and who were moreover under an unusual divine guidance, should at times have risen to the point where their words became worthy to express the heart of the Saviour on these constant human themes.

This connaturality between the prophets and Christ becomes even more evident when we reflect on the parallel circumstances of their lives and His. If a heroic man, who is also eloquent, brave and altruistic, suffers innocently, then apart even from the intervention of God his words will have a particularly striking relevance when we turn from them to consider the Passion of Christ.

For the prophetic vocation does not merely involve a teaching on suffering. The law of this vocation carries the prophet further; he must also suffer. An hour comes for him when his witnessing to the holiness of God will demand its price in his own flesh.

Men, as the prophet shortly discovers, do not bear with a situation where they are called to accounts by the truth. And so the prophet must be corrupted or silenced, according to their logic; or failing these, he must be murdered. And since the first of these alternatives is an illusion of the wicked with regard to the just man, and the second is only a temporary and uneasy peace, the third alternative becomes normative in the course of history. The prophet often dies a martyr. So Jeremiah is kidnaped by his own people, and dies in exile. Isaiah, tradition says, is murdered by a king whose life he censured. Even if the facts of these deaths are unclear, the traditions are significant because they indicate a commonplace of history—men believed that the end of prophetic holiness is death. The prophet is destroyed as witness to the truth which, up to the moment of his death, he has been allowed to serve in poverty, danger and ostracism.

And in all of this, the resonances of the life of Christ strike our minds. Especially on the theme of suffering, as the prophets explored it, we are justified in thinking that the prophet's words reach beyond his own cause and describe the Christ who is to come.

Prophetic Virtue

The presence of the prophet among men, and the hearing he is granted by them, will always be a measure of the religious vitality of a given age. No society can exempt itself from this responsibility of favoring an atmosphere which will allow the truth to be heard. In the best sense, when a prophet is present and is speaking freely he represents the religious spirit of a given society. He is its optimum spirit in action, its optimum virtue.

And all this remains true, even though the prophet may be a cause of embarrassment to his community. Let all his faults be granted; he is impatient with distinction that life makes necessary, he deals abruptly with the cowardly, the recidivist, the compromiser. He is often courageous at the price of necessary prudence, and tends to deal with all situations, even the most religiously neutral or harmless, from a point of view that is narrow and simplicist. He has little patience with the minor premises of life, with human weakness, with other orders of reality than the one he speaks for. From the point of view of men who respect natural values, his views can be exasperating in the extreme.

And yet in spite of all this, the prophet must be heard. For the truth is that he is exercising force in a direction where the majority of men are helpless. He is man of God. And if the other areas of human life—economic, political, cultural—are to survive, men must learn from the prophet those master attitudes which govern all activity that is worthy of the name human.

Most crucial of all these attitudes is a passionate love of the truth. The prophet's devotion to the truth extends in fact to a point of anguish—he cannot understand how it is that man can grant the truth a measure of honor among other enterprises, but never a strict autonomy over life. For himself, he loves moral truth as an apprehension of the truth of being itself. He views himself simply as a witness to the truth of existence centered in God.

And along with his love of the truth, and as corollary to it, the prophet is marked by indifference to the amenities and comforts of life. He has little thought for his own welfare. His strong apprehension of eternity has colored his attitude toward the body and its needs. He senses that he inhabits a flimsy dwelling in this world; and its parable is his own flesh, which he regards with severity and indifference. The body is a good indentured servant of eternity, and nothing more.

In all these attitudes, the prophet is restoring a balance, exerting a pressure opposite to the thought of most men. How few are able to give themselves to God with the passionate dedication of the prophet! When God has named a prophet as His man, when He has bestowed His word on him, He has in fact summoned him dramatically to Himself. And the prophet has had the sublime courage to answer this summons. He has become captive to God's word; he is literally God's man.

It will help us to understand this prophetic self-giving if we see the Word of the Lord as substantially united with the man who speaks it. In the Hebrew view of things, *dabar,* the word, is the vital extension of the prophetic spirit. It goes forth from the prophet bearing his name and the name of the One who granted it. And the prophet's devotion to the Word is of such burning conviction that in a most rigorous sense he stands by what he says, even to the point of suffering and death.

It is worth noting that this seriousness of the Word distinguishes prophetic speech from the speech of most men. Generally, men are willing to play fast and loose with their word, and to make of it, not the larger eloquence of man, but his ape, his anti-self, and finally his enemy. The speech of men is tinged with self-interest and passion; so it keeps the realities of life at a safe distance, where they cannot seriously enter and challenge man's moral neutralism.

But the prophet refuses to leave man to this false peace. He brings the Word of God to bear upon man. He challenges man's slack view of life with the essential seriousness of the Word of God. His object is to put an edge on man's moral sense, to recall to him the truths of existence without which man can be true neither to himself nor to his community nor to the summons of God.

In his serious fidelity to the Word, the prophet in fact repairs man's perennial neglect of God and the human community. His is a vocation which man himself has made necessary. For when we reflect upon the course of history, we learn that the number of men who have loved God or their fellow man in any significant way is not large. And our understanding of the reason for this human failure is deepened when we reflect how profoundly self-love is rooted in man's nature. Man is ruled by an egoism which resists the lessons of history, and the lessons of his own present. This radical selfishness can continue equably on its course of action, even at the sight of the ravages which it works within the community of man.

One would almost be tempted to say that egoism is inevitably present in human life. For selfishness is not merely a choice which man makes among goods external to himself. It is rather the ego of man, choosing in his own favor. To approve his selfishness, man does not answer an invitation outside himself, enticing him from within creation. Even if he silences the world, and gives heed only to his own heart, he will come upon the best of reasons to choose in his own favor—to avoid discomfort, to neglect the neighbor, to win his security at the price of other lives, to refuse the friendship of God.

When we reflect on it, the fact that man is even now and then altruistic must seem a great miracle. To be unselfish he must, in a sense, refuse even to be himself. The word "unselfish" speaks of the void he must create within himself, in order to receive the Word of God. And it is this purification to which the prophet willingly submits, and to which he would lead others.

The Prophet in the Church

In regard to unusual graces in the Church, there will always exist a danger and an opportunity. Paul reminds us of this by implication, when he speaks both of the good and ill effects of the charismatic gifts in the early Church. And history bears out the rightness of an attitude of caution on the part of Church authority when a believer presumes to the task of prophecy in any public way. History is a painful teacher; it reminds us that men who are willing to put unusual gifts to the service of the Church appear only rarely. It is not to be wondered at, then, that within the Church there exists a strong current of conservatism that does not take easily to being instructed or judged, that wishes to "test the spirits" that speak in men. This view of life tends rather to stress the virtues which traditionally have sanctified the body of Christians, and are the "usual" way— obedience, humility and submission.

The difficulties are complicated when one considers the

radically different situation which the prophet in the Church faces, in comparison with the Old Testament prophet. In the Old Testament, the prophet was organ of a new message of God. He communicated a part of an incomplete revelation. God made use of him to record the text of his events and mysteries as these were revealed. In this way the prophet himself became the instrument of revelation as it unfolded in time.

But the situation at present is entirely different. No one can add now to what the Church knows about the divine realities. For God has said His final word about Himself; his revelation is finished in time. And the prophetic function now is restricted to the clarifying and applying of what already lies within the Church's knowledge. So when the prophet appears in the Church, either for the purification of moral life or to announce a new aspect of worship or apostolic action, he stands under the Church's judgment.

Two things then seem worth remarking about the status of the prophet in the new covenant. The first is that his experience is always "in the Church"—it is under an authority superior to the man who receives it. The prophet who would in principle be in revolt against the Church, would by that fact indict himself. For if the prophetic experience is genuine, it leads man to subject himself to the Church. The prophet must be first of all, Catholic. And as history has shown, the tool which God uses in fashioning the prophetic saint is his willingness to endure for a given time both misunderstanding and blindness, and to be judged by those who are perhaps inferior to him in holiness.

The second mark of the genuine New Testament prophet is a view of his vocation as one of service to the Church.

Prophecy is in fact a prelude to action for the sake of the Church. And this action will be of the widest variety. It may stress once more some neglected truth or event (Corpus Christi, as focusing the attention of believers on the Eucharist), or it may systematize and clarify the Church's life of prayer (St. Theresa, St. John of the Cross), or it may encourage some great new departure in the Church— a new concept of the religious life for example (St. Ignatius, Charles de Foucauld). Or finally it may undertake in humble or high places, the endless task of reform within the Church (St. Catherine of Sienna, St. Bernard).

This latter task is perhaps the most difficult of all. It calls for great balance of mind, deep love of the Church, and a spiritual life that does not hesitate to suffer even at the hands of believers. The prophet who is called to this work will realize, moreover, that the first work of reform lies within himself, as son of the Church, and he will continue in this task courageously, sensing the deep current of unity that unites his public task and his personal growth in union with Christ.

With regard to his public task, the prophet will not be a slave merely to the past, or to panaceas and slogans. Being man of the spirit, he will be able to discern realities from their counterfeits, and to go forward in the Spirit. Untouched by rancor, bitterness, or devotion to mere fads, he will labor to make the Church more worthy of Christ. And in this task, certain sources of balanced action must be kept clearly in mind.

The prophet must have first of all an acute sense of authority. One could hardly speak with too strong an emphasis on this point. Recent events within the Church make it necessary to stress again that obedience is the mark of true sonship in the Church. For it is of divine revelation that the power which certain men claim, to speak for God in the Church and to communicate His Word, is the very will of the Father. This claim cannot be weakened or denied without at the same time striking at the divine element in the Church, as Christ has constituted it.

So the prophet will realize that he is the instrument of God's will only if he himself is a man subject to authority. The blessing granted him by authority is his only guarantee in fact that his message is of God. It frees him from lawless, embittered and scandalous tendencies—within himself and within his community. And by submitting to the Church in the sense we speak of, the prophet mysteriously is nourished in the very office to which the Holy Spirit calls him. His heart and mind are granted entrance into a world which is open only to a deep faith—he becomes aware that the appearances of things, and time itself, and human decisions, mask a mystery of which they themselves may be unaware. Paradoxically, his submission to authority gives him new insight into the divine realities which lie at the heart of the Church.

Now to be itself, every truth in the Church must exist in the body of Truth. And by the will of Christ, the Church's principle of authority is balanced by a principle of freedom. The representative of this principle is the prophet in the Church. And strangely enough, the prophet is related to authority as the one who vindicates, defends, and at the same time purifies its claim. For this reason it is true to say that if the Church were to suppress the prophetic spirit in her midst, she would simply cease to be herself.

We can rightly speak then of two orders in the Church—
an official one and a pneumatic one. The former is regu-
latory and normative, and the latter is mainly exploratory.
The first guides, protects and prescribes; the second is venturesome and questioning. The natural atmosphere of the
first is the illumination promised it by the Holy Spirit. The
second, however, must be willing to move forward into a
kind of perplexity, with the consciousness that as the faith
faces life at any given period all the answers are not at
hand to it. This pneumatic order in the Church must be
marked by unusual courage, stemming from a love of the
Church that refuses the usual refuges of men—the past, the
traditional, or the merely safe activities of the present.

The first order is not afraid and need not be, for in the
realm of principle and authority in which it moves, it can
be conscious of the promises of the Holy Spirit, the great
Tecum of Holy Scripture. In its public utterances it can
freely speak of itself as indefectible, as summoning all men
to itself, as the home to which all must come, as the form to
which humanity must assimilate itself. And if at times its
words seem strongly authoritarian, and even proud, the believer knows with St. Bernard that "the Bishop can distinguish the will of Christ from a merely human will—
and herein lies his humility." But the second order must
proceed under a kind of darkness, the hesitancy and sense
of complexity which always accompany an exploration of
the faith, as it seeks to make itself relevant to the life of
man.

So it is always correct in regard to the official Church to
use words like *authoritarian, centrality,* and so on; as long
as these words are spoken "from within the Church," with

a respectful love. So understood, such words express the consciousness in those who rule, as well as in those who obey, of
being one body. And for their part the princes of the Church
who are deeply men of the Church will discern the Spirit
everywhere, and will never stifle His voice, even when It
speaks in unlikely men, or at times and places incon-
venient to good order. And the layman will never refuse,
even in the most trying circumstances, that loyalty to situations which deserves to be called love of the Church. His
loyalty will grow all the more strongly in him because he is
conscious of being respected; not as a mere source of income
or utility, but as one whose human gifts are blessed by Baptism and placed deliberately and in an adult way at the
service of the Church. And his best gifts to the Church, let
us insist, are the same gifts which bring him to distinction
in the world—his intelligence, his largeness of heart, his spirit
of enterprise and altruism. Were the Church to refuse these
adult gifts, she would act to her loss, and even to her peril.

The layman then will be conscious of being irreplaceable
to the Church. On the one hand he will regard his work
there with seriousness. When he speaks, his speech will be
measured and temperate; he will never take advantage of
ambiguous situations to play the truth against itself. He
will refuse to bring to bear upon the Church the harsh or
vicious judgments of men of this world. At the same time
neither expediency nor cowardice will silence him when the
truth is at stake. His motive for speaking or for remaining
silent will in the largest sense be his love of the Church.
And this love tells him that for all his awareness, he is not
the final judge of what the needs of the Church are. He
knows that those needs are present to the heart of God, since

the Church is the spouse of Christ, beloved of the Father. There is One Who judges, One Who knows. And the prophet in the Church will not seek for himself an autonomy which prophecy enjoyed only while men were awaiting the "better things to come."

Finally, when one speaks of different offices in the Church, it is always helpful to add that such distinctions in no sense imply separation, or mutual exclusion. In living organisms, qualities exist as expressions of life; they interpretate, and receive of one another. And in the Church, it is cleric and layman together, listening and speaking, who make the truth of the Word audible and plenary. Neither may be silent or absent. Each must hear the other. And with due respect for different dignities and for differences of temperament and viewpoint, each must presume that the other's words are grounded in love for the Church. It would in fact be a betrayal of one's brethren, and of the good estate of the Church, to allow mistrust or disillusion to pre-empt that charity which is the gift of God to men, and which is destined to radiate most purely among those who form in Christ "a single body."

The Prophet in History

Granted the crucial importance of the prophetic spirit in the Church, it is clear that the presence of the prophet is equivalently a mercy of God, and that his absence or silence is a mark of the decline of the religious life of man. We note in fact that certain periods of the Church which secular history would call great, have been marked by this state of decline. And the word *decline* is accurate, though there may have been a high point of culture evident in many areas—in the arts, in religious temples and music and painting. The Church may have come to an advantageous situation with the state, with her priests even dictating civil policy.

But with all this, the state of affairs in the Church could be called no more than superficially fortunate. Unrest, formalism and injustice were present for all to see. Worship was gone through perfunctorily. The impression was given that certain good and traditional rites must be gotten through for the sake of tradition and decency, so that the business of life might be blessed and its prosperity assured. In such conditions, the public life went forward in the enslavement of the poor, and in privilege and conscienceless wealth for the few.

It takes no great astuteness to see such a period of history as a curse. Church and state are at the mercy of good practical men, formed by this world and leading others in their own direction. Time and this world are regarded as absolutes. They do not lead beyond themselves; at the price of serving men, they exact a slavery from men. And slowly, in all but her immortal essence, the Church begins to approximate this image of the world. She breathes its atmosphere like a poison.

And before her sickness can be cured, it must in a sense worsen. It is only by suffering and penance, and the will to purification, that she can be renewed once more. And in this, the prophet ministered to her. All others had become dangerous or useless. They persuaded her that she was not sick at all, but only become wise.

But in such circumstances it is the prophetic task to insist on the great penitential themes of the Old Testament. Vine and bride and beloved, Israel has sinned. There is only one way to salvation; let her undo the evil she has done in the sight of God. Let her disclaim her sin by expiation. For until she does so, she is unfaithful to God, and unfaithful to the trust which is hers on earth—to be the oracle and dwelling place of God's truth.

But in this message of penance and restoration, the prophetic role is not to be constructed as a mere protest. The prophet is not leading humanity into a desert or a vacuum. Even while he is preaching expiation, the prophet is in a sense the herald of the golden age of man. He himself is the ideal man; he represents a state of things which was meant in God's plan to be the perennial state of mankind. He is simply a son of God who has welcomed his Father into his heart. Therefore the prophet can announce the Kingdom of God on earth. He is man of that kingdom in fact, in hope, and in humiliation. The life of God which animates him is the life force of the kingdom which is to come. But this kingdom which the Saviour called a society of peace, joy, justice, and love is largely unrealized as far as the majority of men are concerned. Men have loved the darkness and have put off indefinitely their submission to the will of the Father. And even this is not the whole sorrowful truth. For the malice of men is so stubbornly rooted that it seeks even to destroy the one who speaks the language of the Kingdom or who strives to make its presence a reality among them. They sense that even a single man of the Kingdom is their implacable enemy, the enemy of the evil which reigns within them.

In such circumstances, the prophet must choose his words

well. Where love and joy might be his instinctive message if the world were uncorrupted, he must rather speak of penance and protest and the threat of divine vengeance. So his word is not that of an expansive and unresisted life; it is a strong reaction of life to the forces of death. In order to be restored, the prophet says, man must first "root out and pull down and destroy and overthrow, and build and plant." The first word of the prophet is the image of the workman overthrowing a useless artifact of man. It is as though a rotten city must be first cleared of its rubble so that new fields might be planted there: the prophet must in a sense reverse the processes of history.

We have suggested that the prophet sheds light on man's vocation within the Church and shows how large the Christian destiny may be. He sums up in fact all that man may hope to become.

He is a figure of the end of things. Across the ruin of lives and the chaos and anguish of this world, the prophet announces a victory. "I am with you always" (Matt. 28:20). The promise of Christ is no generalized or empty statement, but a word announced by One who was already victorious. The word assures man that the will of God will not always be stranger upon the earth. If the prophet is condemned, ostracized, and unheard, this is merely a temporary situation. He will triumph, for God is triumphant, and he is God's man.

In such a figure, the future takes shape in a world that has seen man fall from the hopes of God. And the fact that the prophet is often a figure of defeat is also a mercy of God. For it would do man small benefit to have an Adamic man in his midst, the symbol of a state from which man had irreparably fallen. Such gifts as freedom from anguish, from death and illness and defeat—these would be a sorry equipment for one who must lead men on their dolorous journey toward God.

What men need really is an image of the Man of Sorrows, the One acquainted with sorrow, the innocent One adhering to the will of the Father, the Man of the Kingdom.

The prophet is all these. So he is a figure of whatever man may hope to be. Some day, all men will rise from death in the prophetic image. In man, the law will have yielded to the purity of love. Disunity and friction, of which the prophet has been the harsh occasion, will be ended; the community he labored for and died for, will come into being.

This eschatological aspect of prophecy indicates strongly that the prophet must continue to speak and to be heard in the Church. For the salvation he announces is not solely an individual one. Through him, imperceptibly and painfully, the human race moves toward that eternal life of which he is here and now the humiliated servant.

Meantime, men of good will know that the prophet is the savior of the integrity of Christian life. He proves even "in the wilderness" that Christianity is possible. He continues to demonstrate, against hatred and indifference and blindness, that love may still be triumphant. And by the vitality of his love, the prophet communicates grace and truth to his brothers, forming them in a mysterious fashion to the image of that Christ Who awaits completion in them.

5 All Things New

Redemption and Pentecost

The holiness of God had grown impatient before the pride of the pagan. The hour had come to deliver His people. And this deliverance would show a double aspect of the divine goodness; the justice of God before the Egyptians would be the mercy of God toward Israel.

The deliverance was worked on the night of the "passing over." It was a night that would live forever among believers, making of memory itself a holy of holies to contain His name.

"On the evening of the fourteenth day of Nisan, the whole people of Israel must immolate. . . . That same night they shall eat the roasted flesh [of the lamb] with unleavened bread and bitter herbs" (Ex. 12:6-8). The sacrifice is completed at the feast in which the animal victim will be consumed. Such is the divine provision. And this night of deliverance will be recalled year after year by a ritual of divine institution, to be repeated annually until its fulfillment is announced in Christ's death-victory. Sacrifice, sprinkling of blood, eating of the victim—the future takes shape in the womb of Israel. Her perfection is already sown in her body.

The central act of the Saviour, His death-Resurrection, is thus announced obscurely some 1,900 years before his birth. "The lamb shall be slaughtered during the evening twilight. . . . They shall take some of its blood and apply it to the two doorposts and the lintel of every house in which they partake of the lamb. That same night they shall eat its roasted flesh" (Ex. 12:7).

And when the Saviour appeared, a few believers were able to draw the inference concealed under these rites. At the Jordan bank, John the Baptist recognized the Christ: "Behold the Lamb of God." His act of faith summed up the themes which history had been slowly preparing.

Still, it would be unrealistic to conclude that Israel understood that at the Jordan crossing, her history was reaching its climax. The opposite was true; John was largely unheard. The life of the nation no longer turned, as far as its leadership was concerned, toward prophetic men. Religious life had taken up official residence in Jerusalem, presided over by legalists and men of the letter. The nation did not come to John to learn of the "fulness of time"; it sent delegations to inquire of his credentials.

Indeed, official Israel was sunken in torpor of spirit, consumed with envy of the Roman overlord in her midst. The Lord's preaching must appeal in great part only to the outcast, the poor, the unlettered. And even among these, as He chooses His Twelve, ignorance and formalism are strong. He must warn against their political pretension and envy. And finally, to wash clean the stain of political Jewry, of sacred history despised or ignored, another grace was required. "The Holy Spirit will make all things plain" (John 14:26).

So The Spirit came. The tongues of fire, the noise of winds, were signs of the new creation worked in the death-victory of the Saviour and now communicated to these men, the Church's first sons.

For want of a better term, let us call the grace of Pentecost in the Apostles a sense of sacred history. After Pentecost, the Apostles were in touch with reality in a way which had been simply denied them while they lived under the old dispensation. Pentecost made them men of another age. Their vocation suddenly was made clear to them—and not merely as law, or history, or prophecy. The destiny announced by Pentecost is a Person—it is Christ Jesus, dead and risen, His triumph forming the new creation, His Church.

When the Apostles walked from the upper room, their minds had evacuated the dead past. The grace of Pentecost had freed them from pseudo-history which would declare that the deeds of God were finished.

Indeed, these deeds had newly begun, in their fullness. The Twelve resemble the holy men of Israel's history—but with a difference. For holy patience, waiting and hope, these men had come of age in joy, presence and victory. There was no need for them to command mankind to wait. "It is achieved" (John 19:30). And with regard to the past, there was no need to expose the false religious leaders of the times. They had been pushed to the sidelines of life; they were no longer a mortal danger to the life of man. "The Holy Spirit will prove the world wrong about guilt, about innocence, and about condemnation. About guilt: they do not believe in me. About innocence: I am going home to the Father and you will see me no longer. About condemnation: the Prince of this world stands condemned" (John 16:8-11).

The Apostles suddenly know their immediate past. Through the Lord's public life, they had been coming painfully to this hour. They had dealt with the Lord somewhat like men in a dream. Like men everywhere, they had proven restive and wary under the awakening hand of God. They had fought against the deepening of consciousness which decision brings to men. Miracles, preaching, the radiant force of example, patience, momentary sternness—these had come and gone, and exerted changes which still remained largely unperceived. They were not yet Apostles.

We might say that in the Lord's plan, the years of His presence among them acted on them like some deep-seated seismic shift; a shift that would only reach the surface of consciousness after a long time. The graces of the public life had been offered them in a hundred forms; in community experience, in prayer, in summons to a new order of things. Now suddenly, a public descent of the Spirit released the energies which their life in Christ had been preparing.

And we are led to reflect that grace does not ordinarily violate the laws of man's consciousness. We can consider in regard to Pentecost and the Disciples, three main aspects of man with which grace must deal. We note that man's consciousness is discontinuous and free, and that its depths are ordinarily a mystery to man.

What we note in man, in contrast with the continuum of matter, is a rich discontinuity, a rhythm which allows both for activity and for inactive and reposeful periods. But these periods of quiet are the very opposite of sterile. They are the seed bed of sudden, sometimes heroic, decision. All that seems "unexpected" in man's decisions must be seen in continuity with the energies which his life had been accumulating. In regard to grace, the same pattern seems to follow. Sometimes a holy life may shock us with its sudden turns of paradox; but from within the mystery, things appear far different, far more logical. When we have the advantage of experience, or have read widely in the lives of the saints, holiness is seen as quietly following a course and a logic of its own, which humility or routine had concealed.

In contrast to the stimulus-response law of lower organisms, we note secondly the freedom and spontaneity of man. An observer can discern the poles within which a decision is to be made, but one cannot force, or even predict, the issue. Closer to our point here, grace comes to offer man something entirely unexpected, nothing less than a new level of existence. We must add, though, that grace can do no more than offer itself; it awaits man's freedom. In the case of the Twelve, discipleship led to apostolate, and on to the Lord's death and rising, to Pentecost, to their personal martyrdom, and so to glory. This was the cycle of grace to which they were invited. But each of the phases, to exist at all, had to be entered by a free choice.

Finally, we note the connaturality of grace with man's consciousness. And especially in this regard; the moment of grace must ordinarily await a moment of nature. At crucial stages of his life, man is powerless to accept his destiny if he can summon only his conscious powers to meet it. To be more exact, he is powerless unless his conscious powers also express the substratum of his being. And within this substratum, we must include the accumulated energies of man's remote history, as well as the needs and hopes of his actual community. In this way, the truest decisions of man can be made in favor of all men.

In regard to Pentecost and the Twelve, then, we note how a lengthy, drawn-out preparation had made this moment effective, a gift of God assured of welcome. Included in this preparation would be the shattering events of the previous months, the Passion and victory of the Lord. Then remotely, the preparation of the previous years in His company, the community experience of the public life. And finally, these men had been prepared by many centuries of religious tradition.

As the hour of their grace neared, we can picture their consciousness as a tapering pyramid, gently narrowing toward the top. Its ascending lines mark the great process of Jewish sacred history, from Abraham to the Roman occupation; and its capstone is Pentecost.

Pentecost was a recognition-scene; it enabled the Disciples to know their past. In its light, history swung open like a temple portal; they gazed within, and knew that choice of God which had summoned them and their people. And they knew to what they were summoned. Their minds welcomed a world view we name Christian consciousness.

They understood their future. On the stage of time, the "signs" of Jesus had led beyond themselves to the Church. His risen energies were to expand through their labor and death, into the world, into all time. And the stylus with which the sign of salvation, the *sphragis* of redemption, would be engraved on the gentile world, was themselves. "If any man believe in Me, greater things than I have done, he shall do" (John 14:12). It was His invitation to step to the forefront of humanity; if in Paul's phrase, they were a "new creation," new men, it was because for the first time since Adam's fall, man was now himself.

The nations awaited then. Pentecost was the very opposite of Nirvana. It was ecstasy, but within time. It was the supreme mystical experience of history, but it signified at the same divine stroke the outpouring on the nations of the grace of the Lord's death-victory. We must grasp both terms of the mystery, its contemplative and active graces. The consciousness of the Twelve was strengthened and refined and enlightened in regard to the interior life; but at the same time, they were anointed with the powers of the risen Saviour, for His task. They had received the breath of Jesus, the "Life-giving Spirit."

Men unborn would draw upon the graces of this hour. And they would draw their graces from the Twelve whom Pentecost had created anew, men of the Church.

Now this grace of Pentecost works in two directions. In showing its compatibility with nature, it enters and energizes human life; at the same time, it remains inviolate and transcendent. It will accept man, but it will not be humanized out of existence. In time of sacrifice and setback, as of dazzling apostolic triumph, it will rejoice in making men more human, and at the same time, in making them anew to the Image of God.

So Pentecost will show what a dozen men can hope to accomplish on the stage of this world, and it will show what they cannot hope to do. It will grant them a powerful mastery over time and this world, and it will subject them to the powers of this world. It will make of them sublime mystics, and it will conceal their mystical graces for the most part in lowly service to others. Grace will enable them to raise the dead, but it will also allow them to be put to death, and it will not intervene. In the Apostles, a new intensity of holiness will go hand in hand with pitiful human weakness. When there is question of the growth of the Church, even charismatic graces will be theirs, but the miraculous will never be at the service of their purely temporal needs.

Humanly speaking, the "new man" is of the same structure as the old. Chains afflict Peter, discouragement weighs upon Paul, the "solicitude of all the churches" lies heavily on their hearts. By and large, the apostle comes to know that the Church will flourish in the midst of his own suffering. The lesson of the visionary will be at hand for him; he will realize that he is leading men where they are not fully, or even largely, determined to follow.

At Pentecost two poles of time, united by the death-victory of the Lord, are revealed as one. The sign for the task of the Church to begin, is the word of the Lord at His Ascension: "Go, make disciples of all nations" (Matt. 28:19). But Pentecost, like every divine event, is self-contained—it announces a beginning and an end. The wind and fire are signs both that the task has begun, and that the task is at term. At its inception the work is achieved, for it is of the risen Lord, the Victorious One.

So the gift of the Lord to His men is at once a task and the assurance of the completion of the task. He summons

them to His redemptive work, and He draws them forward
to His return. And during the time between His going and
His return, His death and victory from the atmosphere in
which the Christian lives. His is not a victory that has been
won without labor and sorrow. It is snatched from defeat;
the apostle may live and die as did his Lord, without experiencing a sense of victory. But in his most dolorous hour,
the believer still knows that defeat is not properly a Christian
word; the Church is neither corpse nor keeper of a death
watch. The "good news" is of victory—Christ's and all men's;
and this multiple victory is one.

And in order to lead men to her task, the Church introduces them to her holiest laborers—the Twelve. The Acts
of the Apostles still breathe their vitality and restlessness,
their impatience with the second-rate, the safe, the installed,
the embalmed past. They are forming a Church of youth
and of martyrs. Their church is in no sense an "ideal" one,
unrelated to the weaknesses of men—the account speaks
with candor of the sin and division in the community—but
still, in the main, it is a Church of exhilarating beginnings,
of pioneers with the gifts of the Spirit strongly at work in
them. It is led by men of great vision, daring, enterprise,
and originality. In them, the existence of overpowering
personalities is evident. Indeed, life in the early Church
must have been a sea passage in a small, shaken bark—
shaken not only by storms without, but by the sibylline men
whom the Holy Spirit had chosen: Paul, Peter, John, James.
To discover them is to recover ourselves.

At the Paschal feast, the Church touches their hands—
and the contact forms men and women for whom the word
"apostolic" is not dim with pride of the past, but brings to

her side a cloud of witnesses; men who ruled, witnessed, and died for the truth.

"O holy night!" the Church will sing. Through her memory of the Apostles, the memory of the Church is illumined. In the twelve Pentecostal ones, she knows herself. She is the new Israel. She has not merely taken over the sacred texts by the permissive will of God, as though she were a choice second to some other. But she is born of Israel, with all the rights of the first-born of the family.

And with the sin of Israel in her memory as corrective and reminder, the Church prays to the Holy Spirit to spare her the fate of Israel. Her hymn of Pentecost is more than a generalized prayer against sin in her midst; she prays to fulfill the unachieved destiny of her mother, to be spared her revolt and punishment:

"Without Your divine power, man has nothing of himself, nothing but sin . . . Wash what is stained, refresh what is parched, heal what is wounded; bend the stiff will, warm the indifferent of heart, guide what has strayed before. . . ."

And above all, she prays to be saved from that misreading of history which would amount to a loss of self-consciousness, a madness of religious pride that denied Israel the knowledge of her own vocation.

And what is the vocation of the Church? We are in a better position to speak of it in the light of the Pentecostal mystery, which has impregnated the Church with the light of self-knowledge. The Church is the daughter of God, born of the death-victory of Christ. She is daughter, not now of the promise, but of its fulfillment, daughter of the "new and eternal covenant."

And the God Who chose the Church, created her; indeed, His call was her creation. He did not summon a church already formed out of good intentions, of idealism or of man's hope. But He summoned a people that, with respect to the life of God, simply was not; and of them, He made a people that was. His Word was in the strictest sense, creative of a new reality.

Covenant and Christ

Earlier in history, God had advanced toward Israel. He had come, as the prophets said, like a bridegroom. He had chosen the tenderest of human figures to express His love for the people. The terms of His marriage bond were written by Him. And the alliance which He sought with Israel did not hesitate to remind her of the dust and ashes of which even a bride is made, and to remind her of the holy transcendence of the One Who called. The love of Jahve at once sought and conferred a heightening of her consciousness.

We often see the power which love can exert, in intensifying human life. Indeed, it is true to say that man cannot know himself until he loves, and is loved. And this is because without love, there is literally nothing in man to know. It is love which at once creates the human and delights to embrace it. And this is why love is not only peace and fulfillment, but also terror and anguish. Man naturally seeks to retain the gains he has made over a given time, and to call the future to a halt, even when the future invites him into greater love. Let the future take no shape but the present, is the cry of his being; one has had enough of the sorrows consequent on decision and renunciation, on death to selfishness for the sake of another.

But man cannot be in love and remain in stasis. The "state" of love is a misnomer. Love is an advance; and the bridegroom, gentle as he is, seeks a conquest.

The Bridegroom came to Israel. He came in a stately procession through history. He initiated the marriage bond. He set its terms, He brought it to pass. His was the prevenience. And His bond was His own Word.

Did the bride understand the straitness of that pledge under which Love has willed to place itself? God made Himself bond to His own Word. Having nothing greater to swear by, He swears by Himself. First came the prophets, with a double dignity. They were personally holy, and they spoke in the name of the Lord. And their coming, deepening as it did the consciousness of the bride with the Word of God's love, placed Israel in Advent.

She agreed to the terms of the covenant. Time was not needed for that. Time was necessary so that the greatness of God's love might not be presumed upon. So He delayed. He came when He chose. The alliance was not Israel's; it was His. His delay offered another hint of the form His coming would take, for He is Freedom. The bride can never say, "I have loved You first."

It was a difficult, precarious arrangement. It supposed great reserves of faith and chastity on the part of Israel. And on the part of God it implied a persistent will to love. His love wore the centuries like a garment, saw all else grow old and stale, fill with ennui and disillusion—and still, seeing this, His love did not grow old. So the alliance gave another name to God. He is Patience. "See how I have carried you like the wings of eagles." "I have called you by your name; you are mine." "I have loved you with an everlasting love" (Isaias).

Was this perennial arrangement not sufficient? God was present to Israel in His prophets, the history of the nation was a prolonged evidence of His love. He had sanctified and accepted her worship. On all sides, the people had evidence of His fidelity; in seasons and weathers, in the cycles of nature. Every sacrifice brought the people to remembrance of His deeds; victories, miraculous interventions, food and drink in the desert.

Still, all had not gone well with Israel. She had grown restive with God. If iniquity is a mystery among the nations, what can one say of the mystery of evil in the family of God?

> And He bade me cry the message aloud all through the townships of Juda, all through the streets of Jerusalem. Listen to the terms of this covenant, and keep them well; ever since I rescued them from Egypt I have been adjuring those fathers of yours, day in, day out, to listen to me, and listen they would not. No hearing would they give me, but went each his own way, perverse as ever, till at last I must carry out the threats contained in this covenant, still proclaimed and still defied.
>
> (Jer. 11)

The indictment took a most severe form. Israel sinned against the jealous love of God, Who would have chosen her for bride. But the bride had become a harlot.

> O the dishonor done to thy beauty, when thou didst welcome every passer-by to thy favors, insatiable in thy dalliance! with those lusty neighbors of thine, the Egyptians, thou would play the wanton, those should be My rivals!

. . . Salve is none, says the Lord God, for such a heart as thine, set on following a harlot's ways. . . .

(Ezek. 16)

Still, even iniquity can conceal the presence of God. It illumines His fidelity. "The Lord has sworn an oath, and He will not repent" (Psm. 109:4). As He instigated the covenant, He decreed that its permanence would not depend on so fragile a thing as the constancy of man. Since the covenant was God's faithful love manifest in time, He could not revoke it and be Himself.

But man proved false to his word, again and again. And in the history of the Holiness that remained faithful even to sinners, the believer can see, as he could never have seen in the cluttered pages of gentile history, the meaning of sin.

Sin is an offense against a person, committed by a person. In sinning against the covenant, moreover, man is not uttering a word against an absent king; he cannot hide in the transcendence of God. He sins against Holy Immanence. In covenant, God has made Himself vulnerable. Knowing all that is in man, He nevertheless opens Himself to man, and allows sin to violate a history which in all justice should have been sacred to man's conscience.

In striking at the covenant, man struck against God. For this reason, the Old Testament could speak of sin as a violation of marriage. Man refused the Holy Will which would wed and sanctify him.

And in sinning, man struck at his own future. He set a pattern of behavior that would reject the Holy One when He appeared, and would destroy Him. So the prophets, with their acute sense of history, would speak with vehement anger of the sins of the people. Not only did sin corrupt

man's own present, it conceived an evil fortune for the unborn. For the Jews, a history of sin would amount to a continuing scandal; it would give the Jews of a future century
their cue when the Awaited had come forward with His
claims. We remember how our Lord spoke of the scandal of
Israel's sins in history—sins which were stirring the wills of
His enemies against Him. "You who stone the prophets, and
slay those who are sent to you . . ." (Matt. 23:37). And
He summarized the history of the people in a parable that
spoke of the death of the prophets, whom the King had sent
as His messengers, and the death of the first-born Son,
Whom, as the King hopes, "surely they will respect" (Matt.
21:37).

Through the prophets, God's love continued to protest a
situation which, by all codes of honor and justice, simply
had no right to be. In striking at the covenant, the people
struck at His honor in this world.

But there was a further implication to their sin. The
covenant in Israel was designed to prepare the national conscience and mind for the coming of the Lord to His people.
When the hour struck, God Himself came to announce the
covenant in its fulfillment. He had spoken of His fidelity,
His long sufferance and will to share. But the depths of
His fidelity were still veiled, even to the people who had so
powerful an historical evidence of it. They still must learn
that their God would be one of them.

His name would be Emmanuel. And the most clairvoyant among the ancient Jews had been granted little or no
conception of the way in which He would enter Jewish history. He would be in fact Son of Israel, born of its religious
and cultural forms of life.

He came as Man of the covenant. He was not a foreigner, an importation. He thought the thoughts of His people, and took her words to His lips. He was skilled in that wisdom they revered. In His boyhood, the scribes had borne witness to this. His kinship to the covenant was vindicated in a thousand ways, from circumcision, through temple pilgrimages, Sabbath worship, the keeping of festivals. His attitudes were colored by those of Israel, His imagery and moral teaching were drawn from the law and the prophets. In every point where true sonship of Israel was in question, He might have known no horizons but Israel, no father but Joseph. His robe of Jewry was without seam.

In all that would make one son of Israel, He might have known no existence but His village childhood. His eyes were filled with the landscape of His province; His speech gave Him away for a Galilean. In childhood, in young manhood, He might simply have been growing into an awareness of a Jewish future, so quietly did divine self-revelation match itself to human self-discovery. And if He insisted among men on His personal uniqueness, it was always by a genius which declared the presence of God in the very perfection of the human. It was never recorded, nor could it be, that He was pre-emptory with weakness or impatient with slowness, or that in Him the divinity strode so far ahead of men that it left them outdistanced.

On the contrary, in Him the transcendent God declared Himself from within man. In so doing, He gave men a new intuition of divinity, whose intense love for creation had bridged the spaces between the divine and human.

In choosing the covenant as the form of His religious life, the Lord was reminding men of a truth that is sometimes forgotten when the old covenant is contrasted with the new. His reminder was that the old covenant, imperfect and preparatory as it was, was still able, when faithfully observed, to create holiness. Indeed from the point of view of God's intention, the old covenant had been perfect from the beginning. It was all that a structure of religious life should be; it was interior and creative, a religion of the spirit. Its imperfection did not lie in any radical defect, but simply in the way it must wait on time for its fullness.

Long before Christ came, the prophets and patriarchs had shown what the covenant could accomplish if it were faithfully observed. And now in the Saviour, the universe of men, Jew and gentile alike, must adore a Man of the covenant. His coming was a reproof as well as an invitation. Israel could read in the Saviour's life, the text of that holiness which her covenant was able to create in the lives of all who faithfully observed it.

And it is, finally in death that a man reveals his kinship with his own. Here, it is not merely a question of whether death will find a man faithful. In a more subtle sense, death unveils the radiance of a religious spirit which up to that moment routine or decorum or simple humility have hidden. And in His death, too, the Saviour showed that His great spirit was Jewish. He took over into the "new and eternal covenant" that body and soul of Israel which was His, which was Himself. So His body, dead and risen, became a final reproof and hope to the unbelieving nation. It is in the living presence of Jesus, among us and removed from us, in our midst and ascended to the Father, that the continuity of covenant is most clearly seen.

He had spoken the words of the new covenant. It was

announced in his blood, celebrated in the ritual of bread and wine. And the body broken for men, and the blood shed for their sake, rose again. The risen Jew, Jesus, summons the nation of His birth to the Banquet of the Kingdom.

And He died with the words of the Psalmist on His lips. He did not do this because it would be edifying, or because He wished merely to teach us. He did it because He was dying, Man and Jew, and these were the words which would rise to the mind of a believer in His supreme anguish. But more than this, His last words were a gesture of intense and moving solidarity with His people—a last cry in their direction, a final sounding of the horn of covenant.

During His life, He had been insistent that His role was one of fulfillment. He had come in no sense to destroy. Those accretions to the law which were unworthy of God, He ignored; they simply fell away at His onset. And the fulfillment of law and prophets was no merely legal matter to Him; it was a question of His existence. His vocation, body and soul, passions and emotive life, altruism and teaching and miracle-working—finally, His death and victory, all were ordered to the fullness of His vocation to man. Fulfillment meant perfection of religious life, love manifest, the law corrected and interiorized, holiness given His blessing, the alliance extended to all men. Such were the depths in which His vocation dwelt. And with Resurrection, Pentecost and the believing Church before His mind, He could announce at His death, in accents of victory, "It is achieved."

PART II

1 The Christian and Creation

Christianity implies that a right use of man's universe implies something more than mere conformity to a norm dictated by a moral law. To reduce a Christian synthesis to this would be to grant, in effect, that Christian action in the world is compatible with a devout unbelief.

St. Paul's view of the matter introduces a great contrast. He speaks of man existing and acting "in Christ Jesus." And Paul's central intuition expands into the series of events to which the Christian is invited by the sacramental experience of Baptism and the Eucharist; he is invited to work with Christ, to suffer with Him, to die in Him, to rise in Him. A life of faith leads the Christian into the mysterious cycle that brought Jesus to glory.

And from this process of the Christian mystery, the ma-

terial universe is not excluded. Indeed, it could not be without violating man's nature, which is rooted firmly in time
and this world. So one is not astonished to discover that the
asceticism of Paul includes time and the material universe.
Paul sees all these things as serving the new creation which
Christ has brought into being.

Paul's view is in fact profoundly organic. To him, the
whole fabric of event and decision which we name human
life is woven in Christ. Christianity comes to save man; but
it also comes to bless man's natural urges to create and subdue nature. And this organic view of reality is at the same
time a virile protest against the notion that Christian life
can be divided into formal acts of piety, and more or less
neutral acts demanded by man's nature, his society, or his
instincts.

To Paul, human life is a unity, and the God of Christian
belief is present to every moment of it; "whether you eat or
drink, do all to the glory of God."

Perhaps most believers would accept the Pauline view of
things, in a general way; but it must be added that many
Christians feel themselves rather quickly at a loss when they
begin exploring it.

Let us state a few of the Pauline implications, by way of a
beginning. He declares in sum that man is called to a use of
creation which is an experience "in Christ Jesus." Man's action in this world is a parable, for the Christian recognizes
the simultaneous presence of natural values in themselves,
and the presence of God in his world. All things are good,
and all things bring him to the face of the Father, in Christ
Jesus.

This "right use" is a specifically Christian invitation. For the unbeliever, life goes forward in a material universe that stands sufficient to itself. Right use in life is governed by a pragmatism that admits no permeability in human events or in material creation. If any limiting factor is to be recognized in man's possessions or activity, it is a practical, irreligious altruism which recognizes that men are obliged to live in peace, if they are not to destroy one another.

But the believer must submit to another view of things. He recognizes both time and eternity as present to his being. Eternity is not merely eventually valid, as some reality to be faced at a distant hour. Rather it penetrates time; as the Incarnation reminds us, eternity is present at moments when the human is in process of creating itself.

And time is also a reality. It would be Christian cowardice to act as though it were illusive. Time comes with its own demands on man's fidelity, courage and altruism; in a true sense, his capacity for eternity will be measured by his acceptance of the burdens and labors of time.

Many religious systems show that when either time or eternity is regarded as a separate or self-sufficient reality, it tends to become an absolute. We have only to recall the Eastern systems of thought, in which time is dismissed as an illusion of no consequence to religious-minded man.

And there is a heresy opposite to this whole view of time. It is sponsored by the West. Its symbol is the man of action, the product of money, status, and religious indifference. This man has time for everything except what lies outside time. So his vocabulary is limited to time and this world; it is simply a stranger to God, to worship, to creaturehood, to any reality that would attempt to bring him a realization of existence.

Christianity however invites man in a different direction. It makes time and eternity relative to each other, and each of them relative to human life. Each is present to the believer. The one, time, is sensory and provable; the other is a matter of faith. And it is precisely the actions placed in time that Christians recognize as formative of eternity, here and now.

This Christian synthesis is rather easily set down as a matter of principle. But to put the synthesis to work is quite another matter. It is possible for the Christian either to avoid the implications of Christian action or to empty them of their mystical content. And many Christians act in this way. They feel at heart the subtle drawing power of creation, they recognize the beauty of the universe on all sides; but its radiance always seems a temptation. So they empty their universe of as many "things" as possible. They create a world of their own, in which the purely spiritual alone has honor. And with regard to material life, their tendency is to look at good things with suspicion, and at indifferent things as occasions of evil. And when they bring this mental cast into the realities of life, they tend to act hesitantly, with many reservations and only half a heart.

And this process they call *detachment,* when in fact it is an effort to sublimate a fear psychology into a Christian principle. Such believers have made a permanent state of mind of that Christian purification which is a mere preliminary to union with God. They fear greatly, and what they fear is exactly what they are called to—a love of God which is nourished by a love of creation. It is this violence, drawing their being in two directions, which makes for their anguish. They are afraid of love.

The Christians we speak of are certainly devoted to God's will—they are open to suffering, and they dramatize before the world the struggle of honest men in search of God. And for this, God's blessing lies on them; but they are still far from reaching a solution.

Still another approach to the Christian dilemma might be called the *practical compromise*. Ultimately, in favor of laziness and a want of reflection, some Christians come practically to deny the reality of any conflict at all between the use of this world and the demands of eternity. Life goes forward in such men as a kind of deadening process. They reason that things being what they are, the world being brutal to the weak, one had best keep disturbing realities at a distance. It will not do to be overly concerned about spiritual problems; it reduces one's efficiency, or affects his work adversely. It might even call his practical good sense into question among men.

We have here the solution of the organizational man, of all those who refuse to face suffering as an ingredient of existence, and to reach solutions slowly, at depth. They adapt spiritual living to a business mentality; to quick returns, to a profit motive, to selfishness. They are impatient with mystery. To them the universe is definable by its material appearances, and life must be worked out at a superficial social or practical level.

As a consequence these men view Christianity as implying only a minimal responsibility to God or to the neighbor. And as a result of this impervious selfishness of Christians, even with the best will in the world, their neighbor can see no unity between such lives and their protests of loyalty to God. In the midst of the believing community and with all the means of grace at hand, such men make their peace with this world, and name their arrangement *Christianity*.

The Christians we speak of have in any case reached some sort of solution in life. They have accepted either of two terms as the basis of their solution; creation or God.

Still another type of believer would deny that any solution can be reached at all. He is too sensitive to conclude that time has immobilized God, or placed Him at a distance from life. This Christian is acutely conscious of God as God. At the same time he is conscious of his obligations to creation—to the neighbor, to his state of life. The world makes demands on him, and they are heard. He senses that he is to fulfill himself in and through creation, that this world is more than a handful of dust, or a labyrinth.

A clairvoyant but separatist view of life is the basis of this Christian's predicament. He sees reality as a concatenation of separate values, cut off one from the other. God is apart from his works. The Creator has nothing to say through His creation. If the universe is radiant with beauty, its greatness can be nothing but an ambush, since it has little power to lead the believer to God. The universe is in fact dangerous. Such a Christian sees nothing of the continuity of love, or the permeability of visible things with the divine Image. And since he cannot see these relationships, he pays a double tribute—the living of a double life. He never belongs totally to God or to creation, and in his own merciless judgment, he is condemned never to be himself.

"In all things let them seek God" is a formula which lies in the mainstream of Christian asceticism; it also sums up the humanism of Ignatius Loyola. It may also supply a working clue to a satisfactory resolution of the Christian view of creation.

Among the interpretations of the formula, one would teach that men are to use all things in view of God, by laboring toward singleness of will. It goes without saying that this is a good and traditional Catholic statement of a solution. In the will of believing man, aided by grace, lies a Christian secret—the discernment of God under the forms of this world. Man's will must be purified of the blindness, selfishness and uncharity that would make him unworthy of the holy will of the Father. So man periodically expresses his submissive use of creation by an act of self-offering which includes all the acts and prayer of a given day.

Good as this solution is, there is something that can make one dissatisfied with it. Perhaps it concentrates too exclusively on the integrity of man's will under grace and refuses to grant any permanent value to man's achievements in themselves. It is true to say that man's spiritual faculties must be purified, if he is to be worthy of the Father—but is it the whole truth? What of the works of man in themselves —works that have ennobled the material universe and, in the same process, have made man more human? What of the universe which, at any point of history, wears a new face, because it has been entrusted to man, and because man has been faithful to his charge?

Our question perhaps comes to this: was God's command to "subdue the earth" something like a command not to eat of the fruit of a tree of good and evil in Paradise? If the answer is affirmative, a certain difficulty remains; how is one to explain the adult dignity and seriousness of man's role in the universe? For in the solution under discussion, man's role seems to be meaningless; the only serious moral element in life is in the intention of the God Who commands.

We are allowed to think that something more must be at stake here than an arbitrary command of God. One would rather speak, in a more catholic sense, of the inherent dignity of human tasks in themselves. And these tasks, we are justified in believing, are of such surpassing worth that they contain the mystery of the Father's will, and are in fact man's way to Him.

These statements may lead us to a more satisfying solution. And a better solution is deeply needed. For we know how difficult it is for man to give himself seriously to a work, if he senses that the task is only a temporary stopgap to relieve his boredom or to fill in his time—the kind of task one gives a child to occupy an idle morning. Such an analogy, applied to adult man, seems unworthy of God as well as of man. If man's kingship were without meaning to the God who confers it, no Christian could be a serious worker at all—or if he were, it would be at the price of an intolerable inner violence and the eventual suffocating of his best self.

These are serious difficulties against traditional attitudes. Yet if we pause to consider it, such attitudes as we speak of toward man's temporal life are at the basis of many ascetical writings. The Bible is drawn on to prove that the works of man are a mere fabrication which the hand of eternity will break. The universe offers man nothing, they declare, beyond a testing ground in which he can overcome certain obstacles that threaten him on his passage into eternity. In this workshop he is being tried, not so much in regard to the quality of his work as in the virtues he exercises in this world—patience, blind faith, a sense of eternity, a certain passivity, almost a religious disdain for this world.

Now it is worth insisting that the solution of the purified intention is a valid one, as far as it goes. It is valid because man's union with the Father here below will be the measure of his eternity. And for this union with the Father to exist at all, detachment of the heart of man is indispensable. Only the purified man, that is, will use creation without himself being used up by it, or without deflecting it to the service of egoism.

Still, the question remains of the lengths to which this purification of man's will must go. Is such an ascetical effort meant to rarefy man's life urges out of existence, or to reduce him to a poverty-stricken neutral before great human tasks and opportunities?

Charidin puts our question in this way: "The divinization of our effort by right intention gives a soul to all our actions, but it does not give their body the hope of a resurrection."

And this question of a kind of resurrection of man's temporal works seems crucial. The human task, fulfilled with pride by the believer, is much to the Christian point; so much, in fact, that anything less than a total devotion to his work by a Christian would amount to a betrayal of Christianity itself. This kind of psychic neutralism, even though cultivated in the name of Christian spirituality, ends by emptying time and this world of the meaning which Christianity at its best and most aware has agreed in giving them.

That meaning is a large one, and is deeply personal to each one. One has only to look within himself to realize poignantly the impact the material universe has on man's spiritual being. The material and spiritual worlds are not closed areas to each other; nor are they present to man merely by way of temporary convenience, in a kind of polite and speechless neutrality. The very opposite is true. We have only to think of the faces of those we love, the nuances of their speech, the books that have formed us, the horizons and atmosphere of youth, the friendships which join our lives to others. These things are part of us. So are all impressions and delights which lie outside the senses, too emotionally colored to be mere thought, too deeply imbedded in us to be mere emotion. Without these realities, we feel, we could hardly answer to our own name. And we are right.

Because man is organically one with his world, in a way that lies deeper than psychology can fathom, it becomes evident that the question of a Christian view of creation is most crucial.

Our solution might begin in this way. It is a cardinal principle of the Christian scheme of things, that nothing truly human stands condemned before God. Quite to the contrary. All is accepted and blessed by the regard of the Creator. The Gospels say so, and the Incarnation assures us beyond doubt. Let us only add that the Christian will put hand to his tasks with more courage when he is deeply convinced that this blessing has reached him also, and that in his task he is building something definitive, something that time will not bring down.

We find often enough that unbelievers have a vivid sense of the truth we are speaking of. Many of them put us Christians to the blush, in their devotion to time and its tasks—the tasks of charity, of justice and human unity. We find them convinced of the continuity and worth of the purely human. What they accomplish is, as they deeply believe, part of a historical force, irreversible and not to be resisted, in which they are joined to a great past and move forward to claim the future for man, to grant him mastery of his world.

Now our question is—must the Christian attitude be in opposition to this? Must believers, out of a deeply Christian sense, allow the future to be formed without them? And if Christianity demands in the name of fidelity that the Christian retire from the drama of man, can Christianity itself hope to prosper, when believers are impeded by the sense that eternity is neutral toward everything human—and that if they persist in the forbidden games of time, they do so at peril to their religious faith?

Or rather, are not believers invited, and even commanded, to stand at the center of the human ferment, to direct it with skill, compassion and constancy, and in this way, to welcome and fulfill the human aspirations of unbelievers?

Let us offer a few reflections on these questions, drawn from St. Paul.

Paul sees the material, nonhuman world as created for man, and sharing in man's destiny. In a passage of great power Paul writes of the material world as joined to man's desire for a future that will free him from the slavery of sin and death:

> All creation awaits with eager longing the manifestations of the sons of God. For creation was made subject to vanity not by its own choice, but by the will of Him who made it subject; yet with the hope that creation itself would be delivered from its slavery to corruption, to enjoy the free-

dom that comes with the glory of the children of God. For
we know that all creation groans and travails in pain until
now.

(Rom. 8:19-22)

This world, the Apostle declares in effect, is in a state of
violence. It is torn between two poles of being. It lives in a
provisory state and strains forward to a life it does not yet
possess. Paul does not hesitate to use the powerful figure of
a childbirth to describe the present state of creation; this,
we recall, is a favorite Biblical figure, used by Our Lord
Himself to describe the onset of a new state of being (John
16:21).

Like the body of man which is rooted in material creation, creation itself shares in the destiny of man's spirit. All
creation will know the glory of God.

In regarding material creation, the Christian thinker is
freed from the neutralism and pessimism of the pagan
world. Man, Paul implies, need not ordinarily sacrifice the
material world for the sake of the spiritual. Such a sacrifice
would be valid, not as a cosmic scheme of things, but only
at an individual point of crisis. And this latter is, in the
nature of things, a rather rare exception to the general
course of Christian life.

The Apostle is really insisting that Christ, in liberating
the Christian from eternal death through the graces of his
Resurrection, will bring a kind of salvation to the material
world also.

What this salvation is, we do not know, but we do have a
hint. The strongest validation of the Apostle's idea is the
corporal Resurrection of the Lord; the glorious state of the
risen body of Christ. Cannot we read in the anxious in-

sistence of Our Lord on the reality of his bodily Resurrection some link with the Apostle's teaching here? "Touch and see, that it is not a spirit, but myself" (Luke 24:39). In a true sense, the import of the Resurrection of Christ overleaps its immediate uses. We must in a sense follow on through this central event, and the flesh of Christ in which it occurred. Its very transparence enables the risen body of Christ to act as a mirror in which the believer can read the finalized state of all the universe. "Touch and see that it is I" (John 21:27).

Certainly it is good to learn so early in the Christian era, and from so unimpeachable a source, that Christianity has blessed the best instincts in man. Every man, it would seem, has at one time or another sensed that the material world is something more than a datum or a phenomenon, or even a good servant. The universe is all of these, but it is also something infinitely more mysterious. Perhaps most men feel an intuition in this regard which they cannot easily formulate. It assures them that their relation to the world is not expressed with any great accuracy or completeness by saying that man is a mere spectator at the rhythms and drama of life—the passage of day and night, the seasons, the beauty and truth which confront and invite man everywhere.

Man senses that these things are a kind of insistent parable of his own existence. They bear him in the direction of his own world. They inhabit him. When he witnesses the constancy and infinite variety of the nonhuman world, man is stirred to his depths—not by a mere extrinsic beauty, but by something that is rather in the nature of a recognition. What man sees is, in a true sense, what he is.

And when man turns to the sphere of action, his reflections carry him in the same direction. His place in the unfinished universe is not that of a workman who has no lasting relation to his work. Man senses rather that he simply could not be himself were he lazy or unconcerned or a hireling. He knows that were he to react in this way to the tasks of man, the universe he had failed would take its vengeance on him, and the community of man would be his judge.

In such ways and in others also, man comes to realize that his birth into eternity will come to pass only through the narrow declivities of time and this world. This is a law of nature, gently accepted by the world of redemption also.

This law of man's solidarity with his world has a history too, as Paul indicates. At its creation, the material universe was a faithful mirror of the spiritual state of man. It could not do otherwise than reflect his sonship of God. In its faithful will to serve man's kingship, it reflected who man was.

Then after his fall, creation quite literally turned on man. Its rebellion and opacity reflected once more the changed state of man's being. He could read his loss of sonship in the thorns and thistles, the barren land that met his labors. And in regard to Eve, the parable of rebellious nature went deeper. It penetrated her body, the source of life, with threats of pain and bloodletting. She was to know within herself the simultaneous presence of sorrow and hope which defined the state of the material world. And until the last day, woman would offer to man, in the anguish of childbirth, a vivid image of the state of all creation. On the one hand a new life was promised; on the other, this new life was not yet possessed. The childbirth of the cosmos was a millennial process. Only God knew the hour of its issue—man must suffer and labor on, in hope. He knew only that his hope was not groundless. He had been promised that his universe, and he too, would come to a new birth.

Now it is easy to see, in the light of these reflections, how rightly the Church extends the blessing of Baptism to all material things. In the great sacrament, it is not only man who was saved—it is man's world. The world had been the instrument of his ruin, and it lay with him under the bondage of the devil. We have almost totally lost the intense dramatic terms in which the early Church cast its sacramental action. But a glance at the ritual of Baptism, even in its present mutilated state, will give us pause. For we enter there a world which has accepted the cosmic vision of Paul with an altogether primitive directness. The material elements used in the sacrament must first of all be freed from their cosmic curse—only then do they become the envelope of grace. And as a final stage of things, the new Christian extends the great blessing of the risen Christ over all material creation. The Church blesses the things he eats and wears and uses and creates. He is truly transformed in the image of Christ in a redeemed universe.

This new state of the Christian, however, is not definitive. If one recalls the truth that grace is the perfecting principle of the universe, the victory of Christ is still seen to be partial. The Christian walks in the life of God, but he still knows bodily suffering and illness. Man conquers certain forms of disease to find himself exposed to new ones. As cultures advance, the imminence of death is rendered rather remote, but the threat to man's body is succeeded by a more terrible assault on his spirit. Neurotic illnesses increase, madness and suicide grow more frequent, technological advances cannot hide the appalling waste of human talent, the grinding down of the poor, the amputation of religious and cultural values before the blades of the new paganism.

Man still goes down to death. And the most sanguine of men know that human genius will never remove the sting of mortal death from the world's body. Still, the realism of St. Paul seems to have anticipated all this. The Apostle raises his eyes from the birth pangs of nonhuman creation, to man. And when his eyes meet the face of mortal man, he adds, with a fine edge of irony, "We too who have the fruits of the spirit, we ourselves groan within ourselves, waiting for the redemption of our body" (Rom. 8:23).

Paul's view is the best possible antidote to a denatured or Pollyanna-ish faith. The Church has named herself militant, because the task which Christ has given her to do is not yet done. Let the Christian feel the groans of the new birth in his own flesh. This is only a beginning. He must hear it, strongly and pitifully, in the flesh of the neighbor. When he has heard that cry, perhaps then he is on the verge of something great. He must yet become a Christian, in the only sense worth talking about.

Then if he has heard this first hint of need, this voice of the unborn, his sense of life may be further sharpened. His glance rests on the institutions of man, the forms life takes today, with a new eye. And if his eye is simple and Christian, wherever he turns he will encounter the sufferings of men who are quite literally unborn, and to whose gestation he has been led by the God of mercies.

He sees all about him evidence that the things he be-lieves most deeply are ignored in human life. So he finds, strangely, that the greatest proof to him that the faith must continue to speak to man, "in season and out," is that modern life has in so many cases denied the faith any relevance at all.

Let the Christian look about him. This is the first task of an adult—to wish simply to know his world. He will see there a poverty which is the cause and symptom of the most terrible spiritual impoverishment. He will see groupings of men standing about like broken images, the caricatures of a community. The rich prey upon the poor, the poor prey upon one another. Men are despoiled in body and soul. They are plundered not only of their chance for human decency, but of their right to be themselves—robbed by lying advertising, by a meretricious daily press, by pressures of conformism. He will see men progressively wrung dry of the religious spirit, by a scientific enclave that preaches a corrupt and cheapened messianism.

And the believer will not come on all suffering, or even on the worst suffering, among the poor. He will perhaps find nothing more deeply distressing than modern middle-class and affluent life. For it is not necessarily slum living that creates human waste or spiritual defeat. And at least man could be prepared for the conditions he finds among the destitute. But where material blessings are so abundant, one is shocked to realize that wealth has contributed so little to raise life to any pitch or significance.

Perhaps the Christian adult we speak of had thought once of a religious life that remained at a distance from the sufferings of life. He may even have felt that God's approval of him was synonymous with a kind of superiority to the crudities of modern life. Yet with a growing uneasiness which is really a sign of awakening life, he comes to see that such an arrangement, if it were ever possible, simply is not so now. For the Church to which he is summoned is in the world. And he finds himself swept along in the same direction—the world of men. And if he seeks out guides, he finds that the truest men of the Church have always been deeply and painfully conscious of belonging to their times, to their communities. They are indistinguishable, really, from the other good laborers there. They are committed to this world by the will of its Creator and Redeemer. "Father, I do not ask that you take them out of the world, but that you preserve them from evil" (John 17:15). For Christians are in the world, wrote one of the early apologists, somewhat as the soul is in the body. Without Christians the world is a corpse; and by a like logic, without the world the Christian himself is disembodied.

It is a full-blooded, relevant credo that our hypothetical Christian comes to, with time and grace on his side. This credo understands that devotion to the will of the Father forbids the believer to remain at a distance from the community of man and its sufferings.

We have come, by way of these reflections, to a tentative solution in the matter of a Christian view of the world. And one could venture to say that this solution is both more optimistic and closer to the sources of our faith than those spoken of earlier.

It can be taken as a starting point for the believer, that men are destined for God, in Christ Jesus. This formula offers an organic setting for the process of faith; man submits to the summons of God, is offered the divine life in this world, and comes to the vision of the Father. In relation to the Christian, Christ acts as the One Who summons, and the One Who gives Himself. By kingship, prophecy and priesthood, he claims all men, and all that is in men, for himself.

Let us speak briefly of each of these three, in regard to the Christian. Paul has spoken of the priest Jesus, sitting at the right hand of the Father, offering Him the achievement of His blood—a humanity created anew in the image of His priesthood.

That priesthood, having saved once, saves for all time. The wounds of the victorious Christ are eloquent of this. So we have really two stages of this priestly action of Christ—the one in heaven, the other within time. There corresponds to the sanctuary of earth, Paul says, a heavenly sacrifice that, like a continual uplifting of hands, announces a victory once and for all assured, and beseeches the Father to confer its blessing on the world.

And on earth, there are differing shares in the power of the priest Jesus. The priesthood of believers extends the priesthood of Christ throughout time in the simple will to offer a holy universe to the Father.

The priesthood of Christ is conferred on the Christian in Baptism. And this new holiness must not be considered as a passive gift, merely received and kept intact. Such a view of things is as wrong as it is popular. It is indeed one of the sorrows which the Church must bear—the large number of the baptized who are without resolve or heroism, and who refine selfishness to the point where they do not hesitate even to use the Sacraments in the service of egoism. So they stop life up at its source, with a view of grace that is static and self-defeating.

But the priesthood of Christ makes of the true Christian a giver of life. His baptism has invited him into reality. His holiness has become a source of holiness to others. He simply cannot imagine a universe of grace which is emptied of the neighbor, of natural beauties, of opportunities for growth and self-donation. He does not hide at the altar, or look on the Sacraments as luxuries. He has not constructed a laboratory Christianity, sterilized and immune, but he courageously enters the universe which the Saviour did not hesitate to give his life for, and to create anew. There the believer rejoices in the first victory of life—he has grasped things as they are.

What we might call the second victory of Christianity is his also. He is effective within the world. His life is determined to make a difference in the life of man. And this difference is equivalently the power he has of sanctifying others. He knows that men will not be themselves until they have received the life of the Saviour. But he also knows that this great event must be prepared for, and he is willing to work with patience at even the most thankless preliminary labors.

There is a prelude to the moment when grace is welcomed. And the Christian recognizes this. It is what we might call the moment of the genuinely human. So it is a part of the Christian sense of things to know that wherever the possibility of a truly human life is increased, the work of grace continues. On the other hand, human injustice, hatreds, bigotry, and arrogance are the enemies of grace—and most seriously of all when they proceed from a Christian heart, or exist in a Christian group.

As prophet also, Christ claims all men for Himself. During His mortal life, He was ringed about with pain and the malice of men consequent on His witness to the honor of the Father. And the effort men made to destroy the Word of the Father contained within itself the parable of another crime, equally monstrous, hidden within their wills. The Crucifixion, that is, was a direct affront against the Father. It was the closest human equivalent to the sin of Satan, spiritual, existential, a created effort to alter the state of reality at its roots, in the creature's favor.

The attack on the Son was an attack on the Father. Men moved against the Word of truth which the Son had come to promulgate. And since the gift of the Word to men was the gift of the Father, the enemy was attacking the Father from whom the Word proceeded.

But the silencing of the sacred Word was also its release in the direction of all men. This Word became in Christ's Resurrection the gift of the Father, by which every man was to become witness to God. Man was to communicate, in the image of Christ prophet, "that Word which dwells with the Father." By Baptism this reality is a fulfillment. Men are sons of the Father, in their prophetic role.

We can think, in regard to man's prophetic role, of the intellectual and creative experiences that strengthen his bonds with other men. Man stamps the universe as human and is assured of the reward of the Father. "It was the Father's loving design, centered in Christ, to give history its fulfillment by resuming everything in Him, all that is in

heaven, all that is on earth, summed up in Him" (Eph.
1:10). We are offered here by St. Paul a truly infinite perspective. God will have all the achievements that have
shaped man in time, share in man's victory. A continuing
investigation of the mysteries of the universe is prelude and
accompaniment to the acceptance of eternal life, the gift of
the Father. Man's fidelity to his human task is a sign, even,
of the reception of grace. In this way, man's fidelity offers
grace its vessel. And this Christian vessel is radiant with
prophecy, with God's presence and Word and action.

Faithful and determined, disciplined in the school of human trial and error, the Christian enters life—that life
which is obscure in its self-knowledge, disheartening to those
who love it most, stained with injustice, lust and fear, dread-
ing its own destiny. And he strives manfully to make life
available, to express the divine order which human disorder
can never finally defeat. In this way, by a sanctifying word
and a will to act, the Christian prophet brings a Christian
principle of order into history, into the birth pangs of man's
community. And the new order he announces and labors for
is the Kingdom of God, created by the gift of divine life.

Finally, the kingship of man is perhaps best understood in
the light of the great mandate of the Father that includes all
the tasks of man from Adam to Christ. "Subdue the earth
and make it yours." The material universe brings man forth,
and receives his body into its elements in death. During
man's lifetime, it exists for him; apart from him it is meaningless. It has a destiny only to the extent that it enters his
own. And let us not call this relationship between man and
his universe a haphazard one, to whose outcome man can
remain indifferent. The dominion of man, as we have seen,

shapes man himself—by his excess, by his deficiency, by his constant struggle to maintain a balance of effort and love that will give his life its largest expression and impact.

This kingship of man in the image of the kingship of Christ is also something more than a mere ownership over things. It would be more accurate to say that it is a rightly ordered dominion. And in this sense man's kingship is an image of that mastery over passion and pride of life, which must be his first conquest. His use of the universe will reflect the state of his being. And the dominion he exercises over outward reality will have no greater marvel to show him than the order he has established within himself.

2 Incarnation and Apostolate

St. John's view of Christ is such that he allows the Christian to form a social as well as a personal view of the Incarnation. From the time he begins to speak of the Mystery, John depicts the human race as drawn to God in His Son. The Evangelist opens before men the vocation of the whole Christ to the Father, through mankind's Head, the Word Incarnate. The Word, John says, is not only made flesh, but He dwells among us. And He continually dwells among us, in the prolongation of Himself, His Church. "We have all received something out of His abundance, grace answering to grace" (John 1:16).

It should be stressed that John's view of this union between Christ and mankind is not merely a conclusion drawn from the Mystery. It is the Incarnation itself. The historical event of Christ's coming cannot be called done with, as long as man is born into this world. It continues as sacred history, and its name is the Church.

What John wrote of the vocation of men to Christ was as much the fabric of God's plan as was the human birth of His Son, which introduced the divine into this world. "He dwelt among us" (John 1:14). The Incarnation, a personal event, lingered on as a social event that would unite humanity to the Father in God's Son. This "lingering on," this dwelling among us to the last day, is substantially His Church. This is what John is careful to lead us to.

But the words of John are also a commentary on the historical life of Christ in the flesh. Christ lingered among us, in the first sense, for some thirty years. And He did this not as a statue in a park, or a sacred relic which could found no relations of love, which has nothing to say of itself. But He was Person among persons, carrying on in a serene and human way the work of redemption, the effective exchange of men with their God. He dwelt among us; His birth and His human life were a vocation to all of us.

Now if He were to be fully man, to be one of us, maturity was required of Him. His body and soul required a social knowledge of others. He must put men to the test and allow himself to be put to the test. "Who do men say that I am?" (Matt. 16:13). The answer of men, while wide of the truth, was still an astounding evidence of the reality of His human state. Men were not blinded, that is, by His divinity. But He was so completely man among men that they mistook Him for one of themselves, and no more. "Some say Elias, or one of the prophets" (Matt. 16:14).

So the Incarnation aids us to understand how deeply

rooted in man is his social sense. Man is brother to man in such wise that it is almost impossible for him to learn from himself alone what it is to be human. His ego does not give him sufficient experience of man to draw conclusions that could be called formative. His development as a consequence is stunted or even petrified except for his social experiences. A man, that is, must not only be or act in a solitary way; he must react, must undergo failure, fulfillment, joy, love, even hatred, so that he makes his way through a continual gauntlet of experience that corrects and illumines his judgment of himself.

So we can say reverently that Christ grew more human by being among men; His growth in wisdom truly waited on human encounters. "He advanced in wisdom, age and growth" (Luke 2:52). St. Luke's intuition is of Christ's human growth; Christ came in the depths of His human consciousness to a sharper and more diffused sense of what it was to be man. And this sense was deepened by His subjection to the process of time, as He passed through the lowly arches of hours and days and years. He knew at any given moment what it was to have gotten that far, what it was not to be all that He hoped to be and would be—in knowledge, in social experience, in skills, even in physical height and strength. St. Luke would have us understand that He did not descend suddenly upon men in a blinding rush of divinity. God would not frighten men off or keep them at a distance or steal their freedom away. But God came to them through their own way of becoming; first as a child, then as a boy, then as a man.

As a consequence, the best way to know Christ is neither to paint His image nor to study the images men have made of Him. The Christian way, as Paul realized, is to live "in Him." One must become friend of this sacred Man, in His process of maturing, of advancing from the Child who is God, to the Man who is God.

In this way the Christian "experiences" Christ. He enters literally into another life, another biography.

The Christian has, in an obvious sense, a human biography. He is member of a family and race, and of a given cultural background. He has tastes and dispositions which as life advances lead him with vivid concreteness into his future. He will enter a profession and undergo certain deeply human relationships—civic life, marriage, parenthood. Within a rather large and even exciting framework this is the way human life goes. Materially speaking, it is all rather predictable.

But the Christian has another biography too. There is literally a "way" for us that is strangely intermingled with the events of human life, and at the same time altogether surpasses them. So while we may think of a given man, especially one of unusual force of character, as self-made, yet in the Christian mystery all human decision, the shaping forces of man's existence, must wait upon God.

Now about this Christian way, several things might usefully be recalled. The way was traced first of all, in its essentials, at the time of man's creation. Man was created in the right way. And after the Fall, he was repeatedly reminded that the invitation to live in God was still open before him —God entered into a series of covenants with him. And finally, in Christ, God Himself arrived in our midst to show the distance of the way, the human cost it would exact, the whole process. He went before us. In a manner of speaking

God was saying to man, as a gentle and thoughtful adult would say to a child, You see, the way is possible. And I have even made it joyous and easy, by the power of My love for you.

But even this divine thoughtfulness is not the whole story. For this way along which we are invited is strictly a matter of God's summons of us. We simply have no power to arise and answer of ourselves. We would have to picture the situation as though someone in full health were to exhort a band of helpless cripples to follow him up a mountain. The cripples must first of all be given the power simply to walk, if they are to take the first step on their journey.

And so we were given the power to walk. The invitation along God's way is no merely kind afterthought of God. It includes the courtesies of sustenance along the way, provisions for weariness and discouragement, the interior resources which the hardy as well as the weak find themselves in desperate need of. We name all of this divine thoughtfulness simply *grace*.

But cannot we be more specific about the "way" itself? We can. For we are not to think of the Christian journey as though it were an Old Testament one, made up of adherence to a law, avoidance of image-making, a kind of tribal holiness. The way for the Christian is marked by certain unmistakable "signs." (The word is a Biblical one, borrowed from St. John.) These signs are, in the first place, the Christian Sacraments—stages on the road, consolidating what one has so far accomplished, allowing for revaluation and gratitude and a renewal of energy. Some of these Sacraments bring about a radical change of direction in human life. They introduce one to a new state of life—to manhood, to the marriage partner, to the service of the Church. Others offer periodic nourishment to the spirit—penance and the Eucharist.

But let us think for a moment of something which is common to all the Sacraments. With qualification, it is true that each of them invites the Christian to the "experience" of Christ. Each of them ingrafts man more deeply into the parent life. Viewed from this center, the words of Paul to the Christians at Philippi are seen as something far more meaningful than a simple exhortation. They are rather a statement of the Christian "way," of Christian existence. "Such are the sentiments that ought to be the rule among us, as you have them in your model, Christ Jesus." What follows this great central idea is, we are told, an early Christian hymn. It seems wonderful that the Christians of Philippi not only prayed, but sang from the midst of the Christian experience, of what it meant to be "in Christ Jesus."

> He, divine of nature
> Did not hold jealously
> To His equality with God.
>
> No: He emptied Himself
> Taking the condition of a slave
> And becoming like men.
>
> And conducting Himself like a man
> He humiliated Himself still further
> Being obedient even to death, even to death on a cross.
>
> And so God has exalted Him,
> Has bestowed on Him a name
> Which is above every name

In order that all at the name of Jesus,
Should bend the knee: those in high heaven,
On earth, and in hell

And every tongue should proclaim
That Jesus Christ is the Lord
In the glory of God the Father.
                              (Phil. 2:6-11)

Now we are at the heart of the matter. Believers are to experience Christ by entering those crucial events He submitted to. It was this organic series of events which brought Him, humanly speaking, to the fullness of His vocation as triumphant Saviour of man. As this great hymn of the early Church tells us, Christ entered into the experience of man by Incarnation, Death, Resurrection, and Ascension. From these depths and heights, He earned the sovereign name Lord, victorious One.

The Christian is also to come to the fullness of his vocation in experiencing the events of Christ's human life. And one of the stages for this experience is, as we have seen, the Sacraments. Another one, equally crucial, is the stage of adult Christian action in the world. The apostolate is meant to draw us literally in Christ, to the Father. We are to experience His death and victory as a personal outpouring of our lives, our energies, and our supernatural gifts, at the service of men.

"He emptied Himself" is the key phrase which links the fate of Christ to ours, through apostolic action.

We can perhaps understand the phrase best by considering the ways in which the Incarnation marked the "emptying" of God.

The Son of God Incarnate is not only perfect Man, He is perfectly human. This distinction is not merely a matter of words. Christ is man to the last word, to the last painful or joyful experience of man. This perfection of the state of being man, of all we mean by the word *human*—this in a divine Person is the mystery we name Incarnation.

Now for God to be man means that God has assumed the limitations of man. The Incarnation, that is, declared deliberate limits to the divine will. It brought a new limiting mode to the omnipresence of God. It was an event which gave to the Son of God not only a body, but a dwelling (Nazareth, and Bethlehem) and a name (Jesus, Saviour).

The local limitation of the Son of God means that we can trace His lifetime on a map of this world—His journeyings, His own city. It means that while He was among the Jews He was absent to the pagans. While some heard Him, others did not. While His miracles touched certain lives, they left others untouched. Some were healed, some were restored, others were not. Of all the men who died during His lifetime, we know only of three who were raised from the dead. So the miracles of Christ were a divine limitation as well as an epiphany of the power of God. In God's determination to work through a human body, we can read God's will, a visible text before our eyes saying, There will be no miracles except through these hands or these words. In every case, His transcendent will is humanly evident. "Go, thy son lives . . . Be of good heart . . . Lazarus, come forth."

But the local stage for the Incarnation was not only the homeland of Christ; it was, in a more meaningful way, His own body. "By His wounds we are healed." Where did the

Lord save us? Not so much in Jerusalem or on Calvary, but in this human body, a necessary cause of our redemption. This Sign was set up for the nations to gaze upon. He was taken to an open place, visible from every direction, one to which all eyes could turn, to which all could point. The hinge of all our future became the body of Christ, this body of a certain height and appearance and number of years. Unless He had so emptied Himself, unless our wounds of weariness and anguish were on Him, He could not have saved us. God would have been powerless to help us unless He had become powerless like us. Whatever of ours He had not accepted to Himself, He could not have healed.

Perhaps in this regard it may be helpful to think of those sounds which are out of range of human hearing. They remind us of God, "dwelling in light inaccessible"; what was needed was a divine adjustment to our range of hearing and sight: "The Word was made flesh and dwelt among us."

But the Incarnation also implied a temporal limitation, an "emptying" of God's eternity. The Word was made flesh; He abode among us for some thirty years, and no more. After this a historical end was reached to the drama, a last act. He ascended into heaven, and sits at the right hand of the Father. What remains and acts in our midst, is a new form of His existence. His life is not taken from us, it is only changed, and He lives on in the Church.

And yet during His life among men, He had grown before their eyes, had manifested from year to year the gifts of nature and grace; first He was an infant, then a child, then a man.

Was there not an affront to intelligence here, in this "emptying" of God? Certain early heretics thought so. The hu-

miliation of God was too staggering for man's belief to encompass. The Word had entered too completely into time.
It was too much to ask that this Child in a workman's doorway, grave, unaffected, and normal, be bowed down to. If
only, said the Docetists, He had given us a sign. If only
time were violated, or interrupted, or conquered.

What the heretics asked was of course impossible—they
were asking not a reward for faith, but a sop to human
pride. They could not see that the substance of faith demanded precisely the response they refused to give, that
God's word and no human sign must be the basis of Christian faith.

So in the Son of God Incarnate the laws of growth went
forward, gently and uninterrupted. He entered into time,
and time entered into Him—to form His body, to give Him
a history. "He increased in age, and wisdom and grace."

When we come to contrast the evangelist's account of the
Incarnation with certain pagan versions of the god who appears among men, an instructive contrast is immediately at
hand for us. The myths—Greek, Egyptian, Semitic—reveal
a common longing for a god to come and set the human
situation to rights. Man is searching universally for a divine
remedy to his sickness. But in every case, according to the
myths, the divine one comes as an extension or an enlargement of human powers. Man's myths unwittingly reveal
man's own psychological life, projected. The heroic one
must be larger than life; he is never the one whose dominion
over life paradoxically submits to life, or who can announce
from within time and this world the gift of a new, literally
supernatural life.

And when they speak of the god who comes to men, the

pagans are anxious to have him "make good." The god uses his prerogatives, his divinity, in a quite vulgar sense. The life of the divine one on earth is never a limitation, a slavery, a true entrance upon man's stage.

In fact the human account which the myths represent is not so much a remedy for man's condition, as an escape from it. The god escapes in a thousand ways from the things man finds galling and heartbreaking. He escapes from local limits by spectacular multilocations. He escapes from the temporal limits of man by refusing the humiliating stages of life. If the god comes as an infant or a child, it is always by way of a rather ridiculous mastery over those ages of life—while other children play, he astounds them by his magic. And finally, the god escapes from social limitations of man by transforming man's sorrows into a success story within time.

This god is never "wearied"; he never needs the sustenance of friendship or the sympathy of men. He would never be without "a place to lay his head." All nature is, in a spectacular way, at his service.

But with what a sigh of relief, with what a sense of the genuine, the Christian turns to the gospels. He finds every page striking him with the truth, the completeness of God's coming to us. Here is the integrity of a human figure, the details which sum up the ambiguity, nobility, and sorrow of life. "The Word was made flesh." God took no exceptions, He plotted no detours, He was really one of us.

I look out now upon the sky of a winter morning, the warm sunlight lies on walls and floor, in my ears the cries of children at play. There floods in upon one the sense of creation, the sense of His world. Everywhere man turns, he has fresh evidence of what it is to be man; he is continually led into his universe. And one thinks, This all came home to Christ—voices, light, memories, the sight of faces. Is it not true that every human experience opens before man a larger range of joy and knowledge, and joins him to the experience of Christ? In rejoicing or mourning, in every one of life's encounters, is it not true to say that man meets Christ interiorly? In knowing what it is to be man, we know at the same time something of what it meant to Him to be man. In my joy, I know His joy. I meet Him, to a degree, in all things. In love for creation, man may learn something of the immense joy that radiated from Christ's manhood in apprehending the "work of His hands" (Gen. 1:31).

Now beside being a personal limitation, life among men was also a social limitation for the Son of God.

The effectiveness of the gift of Christ to man depended, in a very true sense, on the capacities of men. Power was required to recognize power, greatness to accept greatness. Guarini writes:

> The weakness of the recipient weakens the donor; it constrains him. Perhaps it is man's weakness which renders God weak. And not only man's natural limitations, but his sin, his incoherence, his balking contrariness. Self-revealing truth needs the will to truth on the part of the listener in order to penetrate. Sanctity demands readiness for sanctity on the part of the one called. Where this is lacking, truth is bound, light obscured, and the embers are smothered. So God left his mantle of irresistibility outside the gates of earth, in order to enter earth in a form that would permit people to close their hearts to him if they so desired. Purposely God limited his illimitable radiance, wrapping Himself in a darkness which enabled man to withstand and even to reject His rays.

We remember that even after He had passed many years among men, the message of Christ had been accepted in only a few cases.

The Disciples remained strong in selfishness and ambition, while the crowds went their way under a corrupt leadership that would submit to no change. We note Our Lord encountering all this blindness with a holy patience. He refused to force the issue; His entrance into the hearts of men preserved a divine sense of respect for them. Delicacy, magnanimity, understanding, met their stupidity and darkness. He had come as brother to man, to the finest shade of tact; and so He would remain. He continued to deal with human situations from within, to accept man on his historical ground, to take account of his pitiful weakness, and simply and humbly to await the hour of grace.

The attitude of Christ stemmed from a deeply human understanding of the analogies that underlie life. As a law of Christ's physical life was one of human growth, so He knew that the mind of man has its season too. Time was necessary for men, as time was necessary for Him, in the appointed work. It would do no good to force men, and only a limited good to command them. The greatest changes, those in the spiritual state of man, are gradual and invisible, determined by a choice that will not be invaded. So God had created man; so in His Son He willed to deal with man.

In so coming to men, with open mind and heart, Christ was able to share the power and the life of God with them. But this sharing of the life of God with men cannot be construed as a mere announcement of the truth, or a preaching. God had not merely come to speak, but to act on man's behalf. And this divine action has its greatest moment in the death and victory of the Incarnate One.

It is as though everything that had gone before His death —the altruism, the divine selflessness evident in the gift of His time, His human energies, His cheerfulness, His willingness to bear with man, to hear him out, to search out with him all the human processes and range of life—all this is to be summed up in an action that would, once and for all, restore and release the human heart. Christ would show His love in death, as He had shown it in life.

And this life and death of His, we must understand, is a continuous history—it is the history of man, the only history man has. It is sacred history, as the Saviour Himself has centered history in Himself. "Come to Me." His life and death and victory mingle with the life of the Church, and draw all the sons of God in one direction, His own. We might picture the life force of Christ as an irresistible stream, an impetuous, constant river of life and adoration and love. And the lives of men cannot run in a direction they themselves have chosen, nor can they merely run parallel to His. They must mingle their waters in Christ's own, draw on His energies, explore His depths, come to His sea—the Father.

What we have said is verified at its purest in the life of the apostle. With him it is true as it was true of Christ, by a rigorous law of the love of the Father, that all life is directed and channeled by a single passion—love of the Father's honor.

And from this single purpose, it becomes true that the apostle cannot be a mere speaker of the word of God, as though speech were all of human life, or as though words, however sincere or holy, could of themselves set human life aright. But the fact is, as St. Paul made clear from his own apostolic experience, that the words of the apostle are very nearly worthless unless they issue from a heart which has suffered with Christ, in hope of rising with Him.

The apostle must be aware that it was a human death, an event which Paul does not hesitate to call a "state of slavery," which finally brought the human race to its painful victory.

And the Christian will never tire of a kind of reverent puzzling in the face of this paradox. Love, which is normally so liberating a force in life, has placed Christ in bondage for our sake. And the Christian will ask: can this be possible? Should not love rather have brought God to us as the divine athlete, announcing a message of joy, leading us to the Father with the strides of a giant?

We are quite possibly back in another form of the dilemma of the Docetists. They were anxious, it will be recalled, to vindicate the transcendence of God. And in their efforts they attached a false purity to the divine which would not allow it to touch human life except by a fabricated externalism. God truly loved man, they would admit, and even to the point where He would go a certain distance toward man. He would produce in man the illusion that He was present to them; He would "appear" among them. But He would not be man.

It was an ingenious theory which had little or nothing to do with the truth. It was a theory which feared the dizzying range of divine love. It was marked by the fear of height to which most human speculation is subject, when men without faith, or with only weak faith, begin to "explain" God. But the Catholic truth went far beyond such pale theorizing. It insisted that in Christ, God was truly and perfectly Man, and that the measure of His love for us was in fact the truth of His Manhood.

Once that fact was firmly in place, one could begin the task of exploring its height and depth, as St. Paul did. No one has spoken of the Incarnation with more calm, realism and insight than he; he is able to enter these paradoxes and deaths simply because, one senses, the truth is all he seeks. And as his vocation developed, he sensed more and more vividly that in the mystery of Christ's vocation lay the master clue to his own.

As the years of his apostolate and prayer went on, the Pauline formula for the apostolic life grew clearer. Such a life was the invitation of the Father to enter the humiliated state of Christ, for the sake of men. Working among men at any period of history, the apostle would come to experience the mystery of Christ, the "slavery" of which Paul spoke so movingly. He would be spared none of its constriction and darkness.

And in regard to the apostolic believer, the same question occurs which we have posed in regard to Christ. How is it that love, normally a liberating and expansive force, puts man in bonds for the sake of men?

Indeed when we speak of the apostle who is deeply conscious of being a man of service in the Church, the ominous phrases which Paul uses in regard to Christ, come to mind once more. "He lowered Himself, becoming obedient unto death" (Phil. 2:8). "God has chosen what the world holds base and contemptible, nay has chosen what is nothing, so as to bring to nothing what is now in being. No human creature was to have any ground for boasting, in the presence of

God" (1 Cor. 1:28, 29). "With Christ, I hang upon the cross, and yet I am alive; or rather, not I; it is Christ that lives in me" (Gal. 2:20). "God forbid that I should make a display of anything, except the cross of our Lord, Jesus Christ, through which the world stands crucified to me, and I to the world" (Gal. 6:14). "For love of Christ I have lost everything, treat everything as refuse, if I may have Christ to my credit" (Phil. 3:8).

And we may venture, following the thought of Paul, to state a central law of the Christian apostolate. The will of the Father, first manifest humanly in the life of Christ, continues its epiphany in the life of man. And this holy will decrees that man's holiness is bestowed and increased in the Church; by laboring there, by suffering there, by dying and rising there. Many elements will form this holiness, will guard its integrity, will conspire to purify it. Other men, personal humiliation, the recurrence of moral faults, all these will slowly purify the apostle of whatever is incompatible in him with the sanctifying will of the Father.

To sum up the apostolic vocation, we may say that the Father's will is to conform the apostolic man to the death of His Son.

There are of course many ironies at work here.

The apostle, working in the Church, is both liberated from temporality and more deeply drawn into the potential of time. We see this in the case of Paul, who would have gladly delayed his entrance into heaven for the sake of the men he labored among, and the blessings he could bring them. So the apostle is freed by his vocation from attraction to this world, and at the same time more deeply involved in it, more alive to man's need, less willing to abandon or give

up for lost those tasks with which he is charged. Purified of
the temporal and local, he is strangely and deeply strengthened in his love for time and this world. One remembered
that St. Bernadine Realino could not die in peace until he
had signed a document making him the patron of his native
town. It was evidence of a profound connaturality between
gifts of nature and grace. The saint realized to the heart the
longing of men for his presence. And this sense of his brethren was not generalized or amorphous; it came to rest on his
own people, his friends and family, whom he would know
and love in eternity as he had known and loved them in time.

We might then summarize briefly the purification of the
apostle in the service of the Church.

Obedience will assign him a time and a place for labor, a
time for beginning and for ending, a measure, a method.
And within his work, he may find that the Word he announces is ignored or abridged by those who hear it. He will
be forced to follow the devious ways which the truth must
travel in men before it reaches their hearts. And he will see
at that moment what codifiers and cowards have done to the
Word of God, how sadly altered it is, how "adjusted" and
infirm.

The apostle will come to know in the course of his work
that the natural values which he had justly considered so
precious—values like good taste, love of refinement, the
cultivation of music and art—these have ceased to be important or to the point. There is simply no time for these things,
in certain crucial lives. In giving himself to men, a man may
even be forced further than this by the apostolate itself; he
may be forced into a mode of life which is relatively crude and
primitive. One thinks of the missioners of history among the

Iroquois, the South Sea Islanders, the Eskimos. And of European and American laymen of today, working among Bedouins, Peruvian Indians, and the country peoples of Mexico. Striving to enter men's lives and cultures and psychology, to be truly a man of the Incarnation, an apostle is allowed to hold to nothing which from the point of view of an effective apostolate is simply expendable.

But the mystery of the purification of the apostle deepens unutterably when we come to consider him in his deepest office, as man of redemption. "By His wounds we are healed" is a liturgical phrase applicable both to Christ and to Christians. What is true of the crucified Christ is true also of the apostle. And this is no chance affair. It is an interior law of the Father's will.

By grace, that "mind" is in the apostle "which was in Christ Jesus." And of Christ, Paul writes that "He lowered Himself, took the form of a slave, and endured a death of shame." This mind, this attitude, a foolishness and stumbling block to unbelievers, is the very grace of the apostolate as far as its mystery may be expressed. The Christian will be a victim, or he will never be an apostle at all. He will stand at the altar, and he will be laid upon the altar. He will be in the Church militant, and he will serve the Church militant. His task of drawing others forward to the victory of Christ will imply his own death, daily.

We are even justified in saying, in the face of the evidence of Christ and of the early Church, that what we speak of is simply inevitable in the Christian scheme of things. We have in Christ a touchstone against which to judge the realism and honesty of Christian life. It is simply the awareness with which a man welcomes the Passion and death of Christ into his life. And the opposite is true too. Lives which remain largely unaffected by suffering and labor, and a sense of the urgency of man's need, cannot in any adult sense be called serious or apostolic.

But suffering, or even the penetration of its meaning, is not the final Word which God has spoken of His Son. If man's involvement in the truth of the Incarnation brings the apostle to the experience of the suffering Christ, this is not all. Christians must not allow the exigencies of the apostolate to bring them to some false form of pessimism. If Christ summons man to suffering it is not because God is opposed to anything in man. Rather we are to understand from the experience of Christ that God is opposed only to "the powers of this darkness"—the multiple forces within man and his world which are the implacable enemy of man himself. It is these forces which, left unchallenged, would destroy man. And the negative work of grace—if such a term is helpful in regard to our subject—is precisely that it arms man to join battle with those forces of death, on their own ground, and to defeat their malignant power.

And their defeat is man's triumph, and Christ's as well. The human nature of the risen Christ, permeated through and through with the radiance of the divinity, shows, like a radiant mirror, all that man is summoned to. Christ is universal man; in Him we are already victorious. In His risen humanity there is nothing but humanity; divinized to be sure, brought to a sublime height of existence, but still the nature of a Man. Though risen and ascended to the Father, He is still one of us; it is through Him we are invited to the Father.

And to speak of the destiny of the apostle, he above all

may take heart in knowing that the fate of Christ is his own. The truth here is as sublime as it is unequivocal. God among men has not come to us as an isolated deity. Rather, His coming has made Him so effectively one of us, that He is in fact our Head, *the* Man, the ideal of all apostolic movement in this world.

The graces of the human nature of Christ were essentially social graces; they were destined, if one may so speak, to put God to the service of men. It was in this way that Christ understood His vocation; the same understanding must be the crown of the apostolate.

> You hail Me as the Master, and the Lord; and you are right; it is what I am. Why then, if I have washed your feet, I who am the Master and the Lord, you in your turn ought to wash each other's feet; I have been setting you an example, which will teach you in your turn to do what I have done for you. Believe me, no slave can be greater than his master, no apostle greater than he by whom he was sent. Now that you know this, blessed are you if you perform it.
> (John 13:13-17)

We are to see the apostolate, then, as a controlled release of the energies of the risen Christ, at the service of the Church. Christ continues to lead all men to His Father, and this sublime process, the inner substance of history itself, is largely accomplished through men. Christ does not will to act only through the Sacraments, invisibly at a baptistry, an altar, a confessional. He acts through certain chosen men, whose gifts have been placed at His service, whose lives have attained the dignity of being named His own.

Historically, these men have been in great part, ordained priests. But the phenomenon of our century, as everyone is aware by now, is the large and growing number of laymen who have taken the burdens and heats of the apostolic day. They are dedicated and aware, filled with a sense of their times and of the Church. They are at work, a quiet ferment everywhere in the world. The choices imposed on them—missionary work, poverty, lack of just recognition or gratitude, the gifts of their intelligence and time and compassion and cheerfulness—all these are conspiring to bring nearer the day of the unity of men and the vindication of God's glory. These modern apostles deserve, in all rigor, the name of men of the Resurrection.

But their lives remind us, too, that in a guilty world the apostolate induces men to ignore or even to obliterate certain human values. We have already spoken of this thorny issue, but its truth becomes the more startling and painful when the apostolic vocation is seen in its full grandeur and is placed realistically in its actual setting. It is, in the stage of this century, a simultaneous experience of the death and resurrection of Christ.

The modern apostolate, that is, does not lead men precisely to a humanism of Nazareth, but to Calvary and the Resurrection. The work of the apostolate—thankless, threatened, subject to suspicion, the occasion even of frictions and divisions— it is this work that reminds the apostle rather constantly that Calvary was the destruction of an innocent Victim. It was an hour which climaxed and drew into one, all the shattering ironies of God's action in history. It was an hour when human hopes were proven groundless, when all natural appeals to hope and faith were useless—there could be neither miracles, nor radiant works, nor peace of heart around the Cross of Christ.

Such an hour did the Father choose in which to act. When the stage of this world had been cleared of all irrelevancies, even of the holiest, then God saved us. At such an hour, when no flesh could glory in His sight, and when faith and hope had died in all hearts but a few, the Son of God announced and brought to birth His new creation. The death of Christ was the supreme moment of His personal and social effectiveness. By such a defeat did God prove Himself victorious.

And this is a hint of the Father's will as it reaches the apostle. The death of the Christian will sum up all the free acts of a lifetime, all the forms of death to which the needs of men had summoned him. His life in the deepest sense had agreed with the death of Christ, and had allowed it free play within his life. In this way the apostle entered effectively into the cycle of the Redemption and became the Father's man of glory; the one who led others, by way of death, to resurrection in Christ Jesus.

3 The First New Men:
The Twelve

Our faith tells us that we are members of a Church which is identical with the Church of the first Apostles. We believe that certain ecclesial graces, once granted to these men by Christ, are still available to us. And since the conversion and death of the Apostles, we believe that these same graces have been offered to men of good will. History, that is, has been a constant evidence of the truth announced by the Son of God.

That history, seen as a merely human process, is ordinarily deceptive and unstable and enormously complex. But in a true sense, since the Incarnation, history has been made obedient to the truth of God. It has served the truth, because grace has entered it to strengthen its judgments and enlighten its decisions to the point where men could see within it the identity of the Church of their times with the Church of Christ.

So we rejoice in this massive continuity of truth and love throughout time. Still, to make our reflections valid, we do well to balance the reality of revelation as a gift with the reality of what we might term a sense of the human. The creation of the Church, that is, might be called, in its historical reality, the creation of twelve men as the first Christians. And their creation was neither instantaneous nor automatic. It was, to the contrary, a gradual and human process. The Apostles came to the "new creation" of which St. Paul speaks, in a human way—by a series of illuminations, by one decision at a time. And this process of grace was initiated and drawn forward by the Lord Himself. In pedagogy, in friendship, and in mysterious rites, He led them into the Church which His death and resurrection were to create.

We must see, then, not only the finished men, the men of Pentecost and of the great Christian awakening of history. We must also see the tentative, unheroic, clumsy men of the early public life. During those first years, they had not thought to question in any significant way what their fate or the fate of the Master in their midst was to be. The works of the Master went on before them with no hint that His works would penetrate beyond Israel into the world. The Twelve were subject in an unthinking way to days and months in His company, to miracles and preaching. Their decisive formative experience was yet to come.

Their lives were not yet sacramental. They had encountered Christ only as preacher and wonderworker, but the risen Lord was not yet manifest. Even the Transfiguration was no more than an episode, with a view toward future events. It was not temporally or redemptively in place, in the sense that it could announce the new creation as already achieved. The Lord showed Himself to them for a moment of glory, in the image He would possess, but "out of due time." So the appearance was only to a very few; and He quickly resumed His normal existence among men.

Then the Twelve underwent the tremendous week of the Lord's Passion-victory. They partook of the Eucharist and witnessed His death and rising. They were closer now to being new men, to being the "Apostles" we commonly think of and invoke. But not yet.

We could name the last few days of our Lord's final Pasch a kind of end of their catechumenate, and their initiation into the beginnings of apostolic life. Accompanying the gift of priesthood and Eucharist, there came a powerful psychological change in the Disciples. They became new men by way of sharing in the defeat of the Master. In a sense, they learned of His defeat by a personal defeat, by that self-discovery which can only come about through personal crisis. Up to that time, they had spoken of the realities of Christian life in high-sounding phrases and claims—a language of egoism and naïveté, with overtones borrowed piecemeal from the religious pretensions around them in official Jewry.

But during Passion week, they experienced both the anguish and exhilaration that always accompany an effort toward personal maturity. If they were to be the first men of a new creation, they must evacuate the detritus of man's past that still lodged in them and resisted all change. As His death was the renunciation by a Man of man's own rebellious past, and this without share in the race's guilt, so their share in His death must be a personal renunciation too, and from the point of view of an acceptance of personal guilt.

So the week began. They partook of the Lord's body in circumstances that were ideally suited for personal experience and crisis. There were overtones of banquet and of death, of joy and sorrow. These men became sharers of a mystery whose full meaning still escaped them. "It is not for you to know, now, what I am doing; but you will understand it afterwards" (John 13:7). And the Lord did not hesitate, even for a rather extended period, to keep their understanding in suspension. He had done it before, in smaller matters; and during this week of His death, He would bring their "slowness of heart and blindness" in regard to His redemptive action to a deliberate crisis. Only suffering and defeat, He knew, would bring their lives to greatness.

He went calmly ahead with the ritual of the Paschal meal. He was content if they were faithful to the graces of the hour—graces which would come to full maturity in them many years after. And as He acted, He thought undoubtedly of the outcome of these lives before Him, the first fruits of His death and victory—of their lives of heroism, their apostolic sufferings and martyrdoms.

So this night was of surpassing import. It would mark the beginning of a cultic life for His own. Certain phrases were about to be made realities—to be with Him, to recognize the Lord, to share His attitudes, to be organically united with Him and with one's brethren. And all these ideas, in order to become Christian realities, needed to undergo a "passage" in His Twelve—a passage by way of His own. How could these men come to know, otherwise, that the Lord was to return to the Father, that His coming in the flesh was not to be a phenomenon buried in history, but was to be matched, and in a sense crowned, by the mystery of His abiding among men? They could not sense, without a gift of God, the shattering paradox that underlay the truth; that the phrase "I return to the Father" (John 17:11) was one with the phrase "I am with you all days" (Matt. 28:20).

These men had known Christ in the flesh, a great thing, a privilege beyond imagining. But this, Paul implies, can be a mere historical accident if it has occurred to a man of weak faith. In the case of the Apostles, this personal knowledge of the Christ was meant to lead beyond itself; it was granted them in fact, in view of their vocation to all men.

They were called first to an encounter with a Man. In Him, faith was demanded. And this faith would be consummated in their acknowledgment of Him as the risen Lord. This is the process of grace which was offered them, a series of organic graces which were creative of the Apostles as such. And the nodal point of their two experiences—knowledge of Christ in the flesh and knowledge of the risen Lord—is what we name the Paschal Mystery.

One day the Twelve would have no difficulty in seeing the risen Lord as identical with the Christ of earlier years. And this clairvoyance was theirs because a liturgical experience had united the two stages of revelation, the period of "signs" and the period of realities and glory.

We sense how large was their final and perfect faith when we understand how diverse were the traditions which had made it up—traditions which the Evangelists preserved with differing emphases. The synoptics had gathered up the traditions about the Christ of Israel, the Man among men. Their witnessing is mainly from this point of view, for many good reasons. But for John and Paul, that bridge has been crossed. Christ is risen, He is "Kurios," the Lord, and forever. He is Head of His Church, one with it. Through the Holy Spirit, the Lord is announced as "dwelling among us." In John and Paul, we sense most fully the riches of the faith which the Twelve had transmitted to the early community.

And with this faith clearly exposed, we come to understand more exactly that the events of the Lord's public life were meant to lead beyond themselves. They were, as John says even of so small a thing as the changing of water into wine at Cana, "signs." These signs announced beforehand the final spiritualization of human existence, to be achieved by the energies of the Resurrection released upon the world.

We have here a truth which the Disciples were to realize with time, and which Origen was to explore with such brilliance. The visible elements of the new world of grace are to be a parable of the invisible. First the visible—the sign, the event, the action—and then, by means of it and through it, to the invisible. First the changing of water into wine, then the Banquet of the Eucharist, in which the good wine of His blood would be given us. First the request of the Lord for a cup of water of the woman at the well, then the promise of living waters, discussed again in the Temple Feast, and finally conferred in the graces of His death. First the discourse on shepherd and sheep, then its multiple fulfillment in the unity and indefectibility of the Church.

In all these parables and signs, and finally by the reality of His death and rising, the stage was set with infinite skill for the gift of the divine Life to men.

How well had the Twelve understood the experience of

those years and days? What did they think of Jesus of Nazareth? We would have to distinguish several crises of growth
—His public life, His death and rising, the descent of the
Holy Spirit. Beyond doubt they advanced from ignorance
to enlightenment, their formation being a matter of months
and even years. But when their personal ministries opened,
they were overflowing vessels of faith and love. The Church
would drink of them without end. They knew all she could
ever know of the mysteries of God. "The Spirit of the Lord
has filled the whole earth" (Wis. 1:7).

And it was through an event which Jesus had undergone,
and through its celebration, that the Twelve came to this.
The event was the Lord's death and victory. The sharing of
the Church in the event was the Eucharist, an entrance into
the graces won for her. And it is important that both the
event and the celebration be understood. The Lord's death
apart from the Eucharist would have remained in a true
sense at a distance from the Church—a fact, an undeniable
evidence of the Lord's love, but still, like any event of history, doomed to the past and not to be made present again
except by way of vivid memory, or writings or preachings.

But through the Eucharist, the Church is in possession of
her central and formative event in an altogether unique
way. She possesses her past together with a power which
allows her to make it present. "Do this for a remembrance
of Me" is hardly a literal translation of the Lord's instruction
to the Church. What He is really inviting her to do is to
make present, here and now, the substance of a past event.
His death-victory is to be announced anew, from her altar.

That death-victory had brought Jesus to glory. It had,
Paul says, conferred a new name on Him—Kurios, the Lord.

And the Church, coming to a full realization of Him, formu-
lated a confession of faith that was extremely brief, and yet
said everything. "Jesus is the Lord" (Phil. 2:11). The formula declared in a summary way, the vocation of the Word
Incarnate to man, and the vocation of humanity to Him.

But this confession did not aim merely to give a statement
of truth, as the Church possessed it. It invited men into
events. God's mercy, as the Church realized, is truth; but it
is also action. "He died and rose again." And as the Lord-
ship of Christ was achieved by way of submission to a cycle
of mysterious events, He invites the Christian in the same
direction. And this is so true, that our religion is fully an
expression of Christ's only if it is also conceived as an invitation to action. *Credo,* we say, but also *introibo.*

Indeed, one enters the faith through a Sacrament which
brings the believer, by way of rational submission to Christ,
into a mysterious death and rising, and through this process
to a share in the work of the Saviour in this world.

It was also by an action that the reality of Christ reached
the Disciples, to transform them into men of the new kingdom. They had been invited to His side through every channel of experience—the senses, psychology, friendship, teaching, experiment in responsibility. And at the end, in Holy
Week, the good news was consummated in a sacramental
experience that strictly transcended all former means, that
actuated their spiritual energies, and united them in a single
apostolic service.

Still, that sacramental climax, from the point of view of a
full Christian formation, would have been unavailing unless
the human needs of these men had been respected over a
rather extended time. Their years with Him had been

strictly necessary. We recall how the Lord had challenged their accepted values during His public life, His harsh judgment of their static religious traditions, the humiliations and successes they had undergone as His messengers to Israel. All these were part of His constant effort to induce mature judgment, and to bring them to a personalized, realistic image of themselves and their world.

With this preparation crowned by the Eucharist, He could look to the graces of Pentecost, and speak with confidence of their future. "The Holy Spirit when He comes, will make plain all I have spoken to you" (John 14:26). The events of the early Church that seem to us so startling and unprecedented, so shattering to the laws of time and psychology, will be more easily understood if we consider the careful preparation that had been devoted to the Disciples. Their lives shed a pentecostal light on the world, because they had first been Eucharistic men. And the Lord of the Eucharist was the true nourishment of their minds and hearts, because they had experienced His friendship, in a supremely human way, throughout the public life.

In sum, the apostolic experience of the Lord was by way of gnosis and the liturgy. Through these two, the Disciples came to understand the unity which underlay the realities of Christ and of the Church.

What we sense as lacking to their liturgy, when we contrast it with later developments, had been supplied from another direction. Simply, it was the Lord Himself, and not His ministers, who conferred sacramental life on them. And when we include in the term "liturgy" here, the pedagogy which had preceded His death, we come to a sense of how rich their life of worship had been.

By gnosis, we understand their deepening knowledge of what Paul would call simply "the Mystery." It includes their realization of Who the Lord was, of His destiny in the flesh consummated by His death and victory, of man's entrance into His life, of the social nature of salvation.

Now of course one cannot separate these two realities, gnosis and liturgy. We are beginning to appreciate more fully a truth of pedagogy which was a commonplace to the method of Christ. It would insist that the best setting for gnosis is the Eucharist. The gnosis, which would correspond in present liturgy to the foremass, is designed to make the Mystery eloquent—to announce some aspect of its endless riches.

As early as Origen, it is interesting to note in this regard that the Church understood Redemption as implying the illumination of man. So one of the favorite ikons of the early Church is that of Christ as teacher. The Christian artists were expressing the truth that in saving us, the Lord had also enlightened us. And very early, by a strong sense of the rightness of things, the foremass, as the gnostic gift of Christ the Prophet, came to be united with the Eucharistic celebration. In this way, the wisdom of the Word was communicated to men throughout a temporal cycle conceived of us as a continuing process of Redemption.

But if, at its earliest, this gnosis was largely unformulated, if it had no declarations in precise scientific phrasing, we know the quality and vigor of that rude faith—its effect on public and private life, its writings, its iconography, its martyrdoms, its hymns—in sum, the new direction it gave to all of human life.

The early Church knew Christ and itself in ways that

seem, historically speaking, remote to us; and we know Him and ourselves in ways that history withheld from them. But rather than lingering over comparisons between the expression of their faith and ours, we do well to note the deficiencies of modern Catholic life, the way in which present opportunities are lost. Every impoverishment of a believer's imaginative life, ignorance of Sacred Scripture, mediocrity in prayer life, obsession with the miraculous, with fringe benefits of sentimentality—all these are the enemies of true knowledge of God, and leave ourselves and the Church the poorer.

By way of contrast to such inferior modes of the faith, we note the adult and sacrificial men whom Pentecost released on the world. The relation of the Apostles to the risen Christ had become, in an altogether startling way, ecclesial. Their sense of Him took the shape of love of the Church. They began to speak of a hierarchic community of brethren, with the risen Lord in its midst, an irresistible force of love and courage.

One must realize that this communal sense was no errant outpouring of sentiment, no mere tactic for keeping the Christ of history somehow present to His Church. Rather, the sense of the Church impregnating these men was the full term of that love which began with their first encounter with "the Master in Israel." He had drawn them, simply, gently and painfully, into a community of love. So their ecclesial love took the realistic and virile form of service—it sensed His presence in the human community, and labored on His behalf there.

When the memoirs of the Apostles began to be written and circulated among the Churches, it was recalled that these men had received two great central instructions with regard to their office as shepherds. They had been commanded to make present the death of the Lord, and to preach His Word. We note how the two lines of action—intensive worship and tireless apostolic action—met and intersected in the life of the early Church. The Eucharist, far from being an individualistic or neutral worship, actually blessed the social task and urged it forward, by elevating it formally and explicitly to God. And the apostolate gave man's worship a body to care for, a guarantee of realism, a view of the neighbor's need as a call to action and intercession.

What was the special quality of the faith, then, in the years between Pentecost and the death of the Apostles? We are certain from the Acts of the Apostles and the letters to the Churches that this Christian love was actualized and renewed by liturgy, and that it knew itself deeply responsible to the body of salvation. It was a love which refused to waste its substance among relics of memory. It moved forward with a sublime realism into time and this world. It was strongly aware of two realities—an unfinished temporal task of the Saviour, and a sense of being present to the Lord of glory. And this simultaneous sense of time and eternity, this motion and stillness, were so strongly present that even while the Church was assembling its memoirs to keep alive the Lord's memory, it was also announcing His presence among the Gentiles.

These early years, we note, did not codify the Mystery of Christ beyond the most primitive and brief formulae. The faith was not yet intellectualized in any true sense. It had as yet only slight experience of the world of pagan thought; Paul is our witness to the lowly quality of the early converts.

Then too, the "Event" in which salvation had reached the world was of such vitality that it continued to awaken human energies and to bring forth men of action. The early Church as a consequence was much like any primitive body; it sensed its identity rather in action than in thought. It saw itself as a family of salvation, in the course of preaching the word of salvation. Without any great effort or reflection it was drawn into the social life of its times to fulfill the mandate of the Lord. Only afterward did it realize that the same mandate of the Lord also enjoined self-analysis, and a formulizing of its faith.

But the later Church, at any given period, will do well to reflect on the work and worship of these early years. Both were expressions of a single rhythm of life, strongly present, strongly and mutually effective. Its task and its worship led the Church to a new intuition of the fullness of the mystery of Christ—of that Church which produces the Eucharist, of that Eucharist which continues to vitalize the Church; both together nourish, form and make present the "Body of Christ."

4 Catholicism and the Intelligence

Catholicity is one of the marks of the Church, as the Church herself has always agreed. And it is true to say by way of corollary that the same quality is also a mark of the intelligence of the believer.

St. Thomas is a good authority in this matter. He wrote that "God has imparted His goodness to created things in such a way that each of them could transmit to the others what it had itself received." And his conclusion is at once a summons and a reproof: "Consequently, those who withdraw from things their own operations, do wrong to the goodness of God." Such men, Thomas implies, offend in fact against justice, since they refuse to God the glory that belongs to Him precisely through His creation—a glory that is destined to be formalized by the mind of man.

"To do justice to God in the order of nature." The saying implies an entire vocation. The Christian, Thomas would seem to say, is summoned to investigate and synthesize the reality which faith and man's nature and the universe open before him.

In regard to this task it would perhaps be helpful to contrast the mind of the Old Testament believer with the Christian mind, as both face their universe. It seems clear, first of all, that the Christian view of the mind has expanded the working area which has been granted to men of the Old Testament. Formerly, certain aspects of truth were forbidden to man because of specific danger to his religious life. We have only to think of the deliberately imposed insularity of the old law, of the restrictions it imposed on man's intellectual and cultural life. The law, issuing from a priestly hegemony, legislated the whole of man's life; it regulated not only specific religious life, but man's social, economic and political life as well.

But the Incarnation has broken the jealously guarded vessel in which the truth had formerly been placed, immune and untouchable. The intelligence of man is now, in St. Paul's phrase, "in Christ." It has a vocation to the world of reality, and this vocation has its center in the vocation of the Son of God to humanity, in such wise that He is the Master Image of intellectual maturity and catholic generosity of mind.

And this relationship of the intellectual task of man to Christ, the early Church seems to have sensed rather quickly; a Christian statement expressive of it was coined by Augustine. He wrote that "nothing is secular save sin"; and the formula of the Middle Ages echoed him. *Valde ama intel-*

lectum: "love the intelligence with a kind of passion."

In the light of the entrance of God upon the human scene, Christians conceded no force to the ancient warnings which had protected Israel. Those warnings had taught in effect that to touch "the outsider" was to be lost. But with Christ, this period of self-protection and isolation is declared ended. The early Fathers of the Church set their faces in another direction. "Welcome the truth," wrote St. Augustine, "wherever it be found, for the truth remains always itself, whatever its source." The sign which had forbidden Israel to enter the Gentile world was removed by the arrival of God among men. When the catholic Christ is present, all such things as fear, exclusiveness, a failure of intellectual sympathy on religious bases—these are once and for all anachronistic.

Instead, as the Church becomes more conscious of herself as destined to welcome all men to Christ, she announces from age to age a universalism of mind and heart. And in this view of the world, she is simply being herself and summoning the mind of man to become itself, in her.

It would seem to follow, then, that intellectual iconoclasm is not a Christian pastime. It belongs rather to a provisory order of things which preceded the Church; to a period when men were children on the earth, and defense was the key to their survival. But mere survival can never define man's adulthood; and a survival psychology can never bring man to maturity.

But the Church, which was the adulthood of man, understood that she had the power of inducing adulthood in her sons. By way of dramatizing this power, Paul and the Fathers of the early Church loved to speak of the foundation of the

Church as the climax of sacred history. At that moment the Jewish veil was rent, and the nations streamed into the sanctuary. The time of jealous guardianship over "our God" was past. So, by a like reasoning, was the childhood of man. The transfer of Jewish liturgical riches to all men was a sign of a great spiritual reality—man had come to age in the Man Christ.

Knowing who he is and to what he is called, man is in a better position, as Christian man, to evaluate his history and to know it for a childhood, which in fact it was. Before the Incarnation, man had been "under teachers," protected, ruled, led by adults. But in Christ, he is called to possess his world in the manner of a mature man; to subdue it and make it humanly serviceable. His sense of the world has been intensified and strengthened, his love of knowledge given focus and blessing. The world "universal" is in fact conferred on him.

His acts of knowledge are to have a new extension, through the synthesis Christianity invites him to. Knowledge is no longer an act which is granted only a religious meaning and goal, as though theology or the law were all of human knowledge.

Old Testament man, by way of contrast, had tended to this very view. His knowledge had been bound to the altar. He had, in his intense sense of the God of Israel, been unable to acknowledge the God of nature, in the sense that there were legitimate areas of knowledge that lay beyond God's revealed Word. So the ancient Jew had come to look on God as a static or even reactionary guardian of the *status quo,* Who jealously protected the intellectual hegemony of a small tribe and ordained that the world of human endeavor should go its own way. For this natural world and its endeavors were inextricably bound up with the abominations of the pagan empires; and it would just as inevitably share in their fate. But for the good Jew, all knowledge was of God's law and God's prophets; and the good Jew would restrict his intellectualism to these.

Such restrictiveness is of course understandable when one considers the destiny of the Jewish nation, and the insistence of God that all human activity be subordinated to that destiny which had brought the nation into being. A religious pressure had been generated from within, by the prophets. It insisted that God was All in all, that the nation was His, that all knowledge was of Him. And the same teaching colored Israel's dealings with her neighbors, and forbade the courtesies and exchange that in other circumstances would have been normal.

But Christianity changed all this. It seems astonishing, when we come on later periods of intellectual sterility in the Church, to note how vitally and soon the Church grasped the truth that the believing mind was invited into all reality.

St. Paul seems to have realized this first. When he turned to the nations, he did so in a way that was courteously knowledgeable in regard to their history and thought. Their literature and philosophy came easily to his lips. He realized with supreme good sense that to come among the gentiles as an alien or censor would prejudice the cause of the faith before it had been given a hearing at all. It is worth emphasizing, moreover, in order to do justice to Paul's greatness of heart, that his love for gentile cultures was no mere tactic; it is part rather of his catholic sense of the rightness of things. His writing is the expression in fact of a mind governed by flexible and instinctive love for "whatever is good, whatever true, whatever of good report."

This was undeniably a natural genius at work, but it was also much more. It was an early expression of what a modern Protestant theologian is pleased to call the great "und" of Catholicism. And he is correct. Paul's sense of Catholicism is syncretist. It has an affinity for any truth of man's mind, as being in fact preparatory to Catholic fullness and a natural climate for the Catholic spirit, which is by instinct open and generous.

Along with Paul, another early genius of the Church merits attention in regard to the intellectual life which the faith encouraged. Origen of Alexandria was among the first to codify and systematize the view of reality we speak of. His school in Egypt, for all its limitations of size and resources, was still a remarkable image of the universal spirit of the Church. And its success was due primarily to the broad sympathies of its master, what we might call his realistic sense of the Church and his own world of thought, and of the effect these two must bring to pass on each other.

At risk of oversimplifying, it would be helpful here to dwell briefly on a few of the key ideas of Origen. His view of Redemption was bold and venturesome. He saw the salvation of mankind as a process of many centuries, during which God had prepared man for His coming. And all the truth and wisdom which man had reached through the world's history was an integral part of this preparation. The material world, history, art and mathematics, had been the teachers of man.

It can easily be sensed how crucial to the Church's universal hope was this largeness of mind, reverently dwelling on pagan intellectual greatness. Such a view made of Christianity, in fact, a welcome fulfillment of everything pagan man had loved and struggled toward for many centuries. It did not merely and abruptly announce Christianity as a transcendent event, unrelated to history; rather, it made man's history a preliminary of the greatest import.

In the light of Origen's view of paganism and Israel as pedagogues of man, the Pauline phrase in regard to the Incarnation, "the fulness of time," takes on a richer meaning. Origen realized, as Newman would realize, that conversion depends not only on the openness of the seeker, but on the sympathy and welcome which the Church is ready to offer him. It depends not only on a pagan preparation for the Church, but on the Church's will to prepare for him. The Church is not to receive man, Origen implies, as though he were a beggar, or as though his love of truth had brought him nothing in the course of bringing him to her.

Origen, being a good historian, was too intelligent to claim too much for the Church. He realized that man, pagan or Christian, finds in his native drives for honor and achievement and self-fulfillment, a full justification for the intellectual life. The fact was clear; there had been great intellectuals in pagan and Jewish antiquity. The tasks of philosophy, of the arts and sciences, had been well and nobly underway before the Church appeared on this earth.

So when she did appear, the Church found men ready to welcome her intellectual faith, and her intellectual view of the world. In regard to learning, she would join herself to a search already brilliantly in progress. In the Mediterranean areas, she saw such human triumphs as mathematics, as-

tronomy, the Greek sense of the tragic, and a Roman love
of law.

And she welcomed these achievements. Nothing could be
clearer; her own schools of rhetoric taught the pagan rhetori-
cians and poets. The early Fathers wove into their homilies
the thought of the pagans. Because she despised nothing and
rejected only what was unworthy of man, the Church was
able to include in her new structure those good stones already quarried and ready for the new architecture of humanity. The greatness of man's thought and history was
mortised to her own.

In the light of this historic tactic, the thought of Origen
can more easily be apprehended. Along with most of the
early intellectuals of the Church, he was convinced of a
principle of history that might be stated something like
this: any great reality that hopes to affect man's history
deeply must appear in that history, only after a long period
of preparation; and this preparation is ordinarily marked
by a succession of foreshadowings and types.

Now it was not to be thought strange that the Church was
subject to this historical law. So Origen dwelt on the ancient
types and images of the Church; he said that these images had
lain both within and outside revelation; both in Israel and
in paganism. Grace had used not only Jewish prophets and
saints for its oracles, but to some degree pagan philosophy
and art also.

Origen wrote of these achievements with the greatest
enthusiasm. He called them a preparation of the nations by
God, through stage after stage of human history. He saw
God at work in all human enterprise; in myth and philoso-

phy, drama, poetry, and art. He spoke of creation as a "scripture of nature." And when he spoke to the Christians on
these matters, it was to remark that the believer has a calm
love of human greatness—a greatness that having awaited
the Church, now formed a part of her visible splendor.

According to the view of Origen, the providence of God
had long been at work before the Church's birth. The
Church had nothing to contribute to long centuries during
which man was struggling to know himself and his world,
and to assimilate his experience into dramatic and scientific
forms.

And even after her coming, the Church, as Origen realized,
is called to encourage and aid the process by which Providence leads men to the truth of their universe. Catholicity,
as she must realize, is an enterprise of enormous breadth.
It leads her to accept and bless the inquiring spirit of man,
to open before his mind the synthetic role of faith.

But Origen's teaching did not go uncontested. Another
view of the Church's role in the world was current in the
first centuries. Tertullian was its impassioned and brilliant
apologist. His preaching and writing form a reminder of the
broad areas of debate which opened up among early believers in regard to a Christian view of man's life.

Tertullian had come to Christianity by way of an explosive adult conversion, and the experience was to leave a lifetime mark on his sensibility. Rhetorical and aggressive, he
granted no place within the Church for nuances of thought
and speech, for philosophy or speculation. Tertullian taught
that the Christian universe was in debt to no one; it had
been strictly self-generating in history. Christianity owed
nothing to human minds or talents, and everything to the

divine gift. And what was true of the Church, was true of the Christian. Conversion, the birth of "the new man," could only come about through the destruction of the old man; the wisest among the pagans came as a beggar to Christianity.

Insisting sternly that nothing of good had existed anterior to the Church, Tertullian added that since she appeared, nothing of good could exist outside her. As a result of this, he contended, the Church's first task in regard to paganism is one of destruction.

For paganism is irremediably impure; and its impurities must be evacuated. Only in this way can the world be brought to realize that it owes everything to the transcendent gift of God.

According to this hypothesis, the Church's birth did not await an hour that would correspond to an hour of human achievement in history, a "fulness of time." Rather, all of history before Christ was a vacuum. The works of the pagans were straw. And to speak of the intellectual life of a converted pagan, if such an enterprise were to be allowed in the Church at all, the new Christian must realize that he has everything to learn anew. For were the Church, by an impossible hypothesis, to allow her waters to mingle with those of the pagan mind, the purity of her message could not but be contaminated.

In reading Tertullian, one remarks that in spite of all his zeal he is victim of a rather constant tendency to canonize personal experience. He exemplifies, even, a kind of churchman's arrogance which makes of personal psychology and views, the mind of the Church. An explosive conversion and a fiery temperament had generated the heated extremism so evident whenever the question of conversion arises in his writings. He could not bear the thought that the Church might be more generous and open than he.

But the Catholic mind is in fact more generous, and the mystery of conversion more complex, than Tertullian could imagine. Newman was to sense this. The newness of Christianity, he saw, does not consist in a transcendence which is a mere apartness from history. Rather, Catholic newness is summed up in the understanding which she gives to the pivotal word *sacred.*

With her, the sacred is defined from the vantage point of the Incarnation. And the Incarnation is neither rootless nor timeless with regard to human life. It is in truth the finest moment of human history itself, by the gift of God. It is a true moment of time, a moment of decision and love, an act of God brought to pass within man's world.

And from this intuition of the Church, a double rhythm is induced in the world. The Church impregnates creation with the life of God, and she welcomes its human values into the regimen of grace. So when the Church invites believing men to the tasks of the mind, she is able to introduce a new synthetic element into human thought. The revelation of God with regard to the Christian mysteries is transcendent and absolute, but with regard to things human— knowledge, artistic life, cultures, it is immanent, permeating and unitive. In this way, faith not only introduces man to a world of mystery, but illumines and orders the areas of human knowledge common to all men.

We have said that the Church was not the first to invite man's intelligence to enter and take possession of reality. And the Christian is not embarrassed by allowing that this task could conceivably have gone forward without the Church, as the task had in fact begun before the Church existed. He knows that even if the Church had not yet appeared, man could conceivably have reached his present state of cultural and scientific manhood. All this one can grant as possible; it is simply not to the point here.

To the point is the intellectual achievement of the Church in history. She is the only one among the world religions to banish from her presence the secular principle. At no time in her history would she have part in the idea that the world is closed off from her; that she has nothing to offer man's thought or that the genius of man brings no gift to her. In principle, she could not tolerate a merely passive presence to the world of man's thought, or a religious toleration of it, or the assumption that religious faith is a stranger to the mind and its works.

The forms of secularism which the Church fought in history are so multiple that we are justified in speaking of them not merely as historical phenomena, but as constant temptations of man. Some of these forms arose from paganism, others from within the Church itself—Gnosticism, Pelagianism, Jansenism—but all of them were built upon a principle of exclusion. They fought for a world without the Church, or a Church without the world. And but for the Church's awareness of the crucial nature of this struggle, secularism would long since have won the day.

It did not win, as history is witness. And in this struggle, and in the successive victories she won, it is worth stressing that the Church was acting not simply for herself, but for man. She was vindicating man's soul, in one or another way. At one time, it was from a pernicious optimism that declared man capable of coming to the life of God by his own powers of altruism or pride. At another time she won against a despair that would grant evil an honored place in the universe, and put the outcome of man's struggle in jeopardy by striking at his hope. Again, she fought the idea that creation was corrupt, or that nature was man's enemy.

She was struggling, really, against one or another form of the principle of exclusion, on behalf of catholicity. She was struggling for the right to be herself, and in so being, to allow man to exist as himself, freed from the slaveries which man's own thought had forged.

It need hardly be said that the struggle of the Church continues today. And its present situation invites us not so much to a tallying of gains, as to a simple and dolorous hope.

For to say the least, the march of events cannot be called favorable to the Church. It is sufficient to recall the last four or five hundred years of history in order to realize the truth of this. Those years saw three stages of effective opposition which have succeeded in reducing the body of ancient "Christendom" to a more or less ineffectual minority. The first stage was the destruction of inner unity. The second tended to cast doubt on the relevance of religion to society. And the third, accepting this state of affairs in its turn, was inclined to reject even the idea of a private witnessing in religious life.

And along with these changes we note the break-up of the organic components of man's life: science from culture, politics and public life from morality, and as if by implicit agreement, all of these together from the life of man in God. In this way, not only the relevance of faith but its very right to exist have become matters for sober debate.

It requires a great deal of vitality, one would agree, for the religious spirit of man even to exist under such a situation. But to press the public claim of religion, no matter how acutely these are felt, would seem to be folly. Yet the pressing of this claim, in season and out, remains a substantial part of the Christian task.

The believer's sense of his times moreover will forbid him, with regard to the state of his faith, to name the times incurably hostile or irreparable. The terms are unrealistic and simply unhistorical. The fact is that there have been better times, and there have been worse times, and probably the most deceptive judgment on any period of history comes from those who are within it. The Christian historical sense suggests rather that the present is by no means as evil as it appears, nor is the past as attractive as our remoteness from it would make it seem.

Knowing history, the Christian can regard his own times with the detached love necessary to him if he is to work effectively in them. His faith tells him that the only reality promised and indefectible life within time is the Church itself. The promise of Christ is extended to nothing else; neither to forms of government nor to treaties made with the Church, nor to cultures favorable or inimical to her, nor even to special forms of the religious vocation. All forms and groupings of man are by nature subject to change and to death; no matter what philosophy of history one prefers, the fact is clear, as theology tells us. For the Christian adult, these facts are at once sobering and encouraging.

His sense of history gives a fine edge of discernment to his view of life. He knows the difference for instance between serving the Church and trying to make her, even with the best will in the world, acceptable to this or that age. He is strong in a sense of mystery, as he is strong in the sense of his life's task. So he can see the ambiguities which are bound to be present when the Church is triumphant within time, just as he can live equably in an age when the Church is in a minor role or must submit to persecution.

And if he is a Christian living today, he finds in the Church's contemporary struggle the greatest stimulus to his loyalty and zeal. He knows that defeats are not irreversible, as though the Church were a victim of some blind circle of time or were bound to a Will that allowed no free play to the will of man. Christian theology is agreed that the onset of modern paganism can be turned back by holy and zealous men; and turned back on the same three stages of its apparent triumph—man's conscience, public life, and the unity of the nations. The moment when public life lost its roots in religious life is reversed by the moment when a viable religious life communicates its spirit once more to the life of man.

Again, we have our lesson from history. It is instructive that the modern break-up of religious unity began not from without but from within the Church. The Church had shown in a hundred previous crises that her vitality could summon resources to meet her enemies. But at a point of time, she was unable to put to good use the reforming zeal of some of her own members. The spirit of reform was embittered, and broke away. This is an aspect of the historical truth which Catholics have not often dwelt upon; but as Pope

John has said, Catholics must bear a part of the blame for the loss of religious unity. The Catholic spirit, a welcoming of the truth even when the truth is unpleasant and insistent, has not always been part of the equipment of Christian men.

A simple sense of history will tell us that the modern religious situation is at least partially the historic outcome of this Christian failure. The Church of the sixteenth century had refused a hearing to believers who were reacting against selfishness and clericalism and worldliness. We are not forbidden, then, to see the beginnings of the revolt as a profound religious reaction to abuses within the Church. In many of its first aspects the reform had been admirable and holy.

It remains true nonetheless that the Reformation came eventually to a principle, not of reform, but of division, and that it set in motion the beginnings of a debate whose progress went somewhat as we have indicated. First, the public worth of religion was called into question; then the intelligence of man began seriously to doubt the very worth of religion to human life.

The theological doubtings of man, in one form or another, go on. Analyzed and psychoanalyzed and elaborated in symbols, they are the source of much of the greatness of modern literature. It would not be far from the truth to say that one who does not understand the power which religious doubt exerts in the spiritual life of modern man will have little understanding of him at all. One thinks almost at random of Newman, Claudel, Rouault, Lorca, Brunner, Greene, de Foucauld—of those whose religious and ideological and literary judgments have shaped man's spirit today. It is through this fearless and agonized inner debate, in which the meaning of existence itself was sometimes placed in the balance, that their achievement was formed.

And what draws all men irresistibly toward them is something much more than the triumphant outcome of their struggle. It is rather the vitality of their struggle itself, the power and honesty with which its terms are illuminated. It is modern man's fascination, not for goals and victories, but for "the way," for struggle and the ironies of combat.

If there is anything in all this that remains regrettable, it is not a debate which has given modern history so many of its great spirits. For this, man can only be grateful. But the truly regrettable fact is that the debate is conducted in many instances so unfairly. The state of the question in regard to the nature and value of religious faith is weighted with half truths and fables and prejudices, and the burden of historical Christian failure. The debaters show a genius for the peripheral, for ignoring what is central. They disinter buried issues, substitute rancor for human feelings, and call it religious conversation.

Still, at the heart of these failures lies a Christian opportunity. The Christian intellectual, that is, accepts as his task the restoration of an atmosphere of life in which the claims of the faith may win a hearing. The task rightly understood is a public one and an intellectual one. One cannot be true to it and cast about to affect one or another individual while his environment, with its many complicated structures, remains untouched. Neither is one stating the terms of the task with any accuracy by viewing it as some kind of intellectual violence. The task is rather to give a quiet and persistent evidence of the great idea that the sacred is not a threat to man, that the truest victories of man's spirit are consonant with belief, and that modern man loses neither his claims nor his ambition nor his honor before men, by an act of faith.

5 Sacrifice and Man's Hope

It is clear from the Old Testament that God's historical promises to man were reducibly two. They included the blessing of lands and progeny, as guarantees of an eventual blessing of the Messiah. And in return, as Scripture makes clear, the people bound themselves to God in an obedient love.

It is notable that in both aspects of this covenant—God's promise and man's response—man's sense of existence is heightened. By one agreement, God reveals His nature, and men are taught the definition of man. Essential relationships are set up—between God and man, between man and man.

It is not enough, however, that God should set up these relationships *in vacuo,* as though history were reducible to a set of abstract propositions. A merely juridic agreement with God would be useless to most men; the majority of them are not learned, and even the learned need to have the power of their minds released by immersing them in a dramatic action. Otherwise, the threat is that the ignorant will gain no sense of their identity or history; and the intellectual will yield to sterility and abstractionism, to a religion of mere gesture.

Sacrifice enters the religious scene to guard against both threats. And a measure of the dramatic value of sacrifice is its early appearance in history. It is as though the need of performing sacrifice were imbedded in man. And indeed it is. Sacrificial rites remind man, by a most powerful pedagogy, of two realities; of the identity of both God and man. And this reminder comes through an action which brings the shaping events of his history again before men and makes his past greatness available to him.

But what exactly does man sacrifice to God?

We could begin by saying that God has revealed Himself to men, first of all as Benefactor. His goodness reaches man in the free gift of existence, and culminates in eternal life with God. To this term, all rational existence is ordered. And the material universe, faith tells us, is to be of use in this process of history; its noblest use culminates in its power of illustrating man's existence. It is the means which, when brought to his worship, takes the shape of a dramatic symbol in action.

Even prior to the old covenant, God as Benefactor appeared to man—One Who protected man from his enemies and guaranteed the order of the physical universe in its circuit of seasons and days.

But God's providence did not exhaust itself in these two

benefits. He offered the Jews a more important blessing by far: a place in history which could be called sacred. Israel was the sacred servant of the continuity of divine event; its sons were men of sacred history. As such they were blessed in all their generations because they not merely transmitted life in the biological sense, they penetrated to the realities signified by this world and its processes. In so doing, they made life itself into an instrument of God's action in time.

Indeed the other nations outside Israel had meaning in history only in relation to the people of God. The gentiles were either instruments of God's chastisement of His people, or parables of the vanity of faithless temporal power.

But God's people had a central place. And this "placing" of them by God is the very opposite of a mere *status quo*. For God shows in them His delight in acting unexpectedly in time. He shows that the divine Mind, while reflected in human categories, is utterly transcendent to time and creation. It is a Knowledge that includes present, past, and future in one Act, and so is able to order and perfect all of time to His purposes.

The unexpected acts through nature and above nature. It acts by way of tender regard for the material needs of men, and by way of abrupt disregard of them; by way of the cycles of time and the rupture of cycles; through the mouth of nature and the mouth of the prophet. It does not scorn the lowliest teaching tool—the visible world of time. And it does not hesitate to claim the noblest tool of all—the mind and heart of the saint.

Now it was at sacrifice that man's recognition of his Benefactor was given its most vivid setting from the beginning of man's religious history. Along with a renewal of obedience and gratitude, the Jewish community at sacrificial worship renewed its sense of destiny—one might almost say, its sense of being history—of being the sacred creation of God, His people.

A few words on sacrifice might be of help here. Sacrifice is the noblest possible use of nature, since through it, nature's irrationality and opaqueness are corrected by man's sense of purpose. It is at sacrifice, in short, that he formally elevates all visible things—harvest, animals, oil, wine—to the uses of adoration.

It is the simplest of actions, in the days when religious spirit is most genuine. But humble and primitive though it be, the action has within itself, by its evocative power, the strength to bring the adoring community to an acceptance of its destiny. And this openness to destiny implies, in turn, openness to the God Who is man's Benefactor, Who summons men. Sacrifice assures man that the God Who created, blessed, gave man a prophecy and priesthood, will not cease these great divine acts in time; that man's history will not cease to be sacred.

And the assurance of God's blessing comes about, strangely enough, within an action which makes use of this world as the vehicle of its adoration. At sacrifice, the material world is borne upward toward God; it assumes the sublime power of expressing man's deepest consciousness. It rises to God as the sign of man's response to the blessings of temporal and eternal life.

Memory and acceptance and hope—these three poles of man's consciousness are made luminous at sacrifice.

In the memory of past greatness man finds a chief stimulant to his present community life. At the beginning of sacred history, men had to forge for themselves, out of opportunity and setback and with little beside the divine promise to lead them forward, those achievements which were determinant of the future. But as history gathers momentum, the nation finds that its store of memories has an enormous power to strengthen its sense of identity and bring it to a common action. The Jews went through Exodus and the salvific acts of God in the desert, and a communal liturgy makes these acts live again. In this way the past is still alive and available. In community consciousness the people find its great men still present, recalled explicitly at given times by community ritual, to meet a need of crisis or an occasion of rejoicing.

In this regard, what man has to mourn in contemporary life is the absence of viable memory as a stratum of consciousness. Great heroic types are lost in the past: without this nourishment of example to draw on, the people are inevitably impoverished. The riches of history are squandered; men are forced to create anew what the past has already in fact created for them, but which a loss of the traditional sense has deprived them of.

In Israel, the recurring sacrifices brought to mind the substance of a great past—the men of the patriarchal age, their faith and steadfastness and charity, and especially those great moments when, by choosing in God's favor, they turned the future of their people in His direction. Abraham's faith, as Paul reminds us, became the instrument of God in the fashioning of His people. More than this, the patriarch's holy willingness to sacrifice his son was a type of the divine Fatherhood, in its gift of the Redeemer. The choice that Abraham made in God's favor so overreached the life of man as to become an image of all heroic choices of history.

Along with the past, the people's sense of the present is of course crucial to it. If the past is a matrix of God's will in time, the present is its epiphany. And the virile will to accept the present becomes for the individual, or the community, a criterion of spiritual vitality. Whether the present is prosperous or not, the triumph of faith is man's ability to discern the divine Presence in his world. And in both setback and good favor, religious man may discover that the will of God is equally his Benefactor. Whether God blesses or reproves the forms of human life, that life is in fact going forward under His providential will. This is something of what we commonly mean by a believing sense of the present.

In sacrifice, this religious meaning of the "now" is clarified. The gestures and prayers and actions of the ritual give point to the belief that all creation expresses present existence before the face of God. If ever man is to be himself, personally and socially, it is now. His life is dramatized by a direct, sincere action rooted humbly in the world of nature and expressive of his longing to welcome God to the human scene.

A given present may be governed by a sense of communal guilt. The symbolic death of the animal will set things aright again—not of itself, but in dramatizing before the people their spiritual chaos and awakening them to a saving repentence. "God," the sacred author implies, "was pleased on that day." It is a human way of expressing the unity which the rite established between the will of God and the refashioning of men's hearts. After their sacrifice, men were set firmly again in the direction of their first duty. They had recovered their sense of creaturehood.

Or perhaps at a given moment, the people are suffering under temporal misfortune. This is a moment both of danger and opportunity; it can germinate a sense of revolt in men, or can symbolize a passage of grace. But deliberately to choose an animal from the flock, to slay it before the community, to let its blood run out—in this men may read the meaning that underlies suffering. For in the animal death before them, the spiritual death demanded of them is being dramatized. Carnal death is the parable of spiritual death; and fallen men read in mactation a summons to that purification without which man cannot enter before the living God. Visible sacrifice leads man inward, to the extinction of his sufficiency and pride.

This is the clue to the sealing of the covenant, enacted by Moses and the people in the desert. Sacrifice was to draw the community to a religious state of being. For this purpose an admirable structure of worship is promulgated at Sinai, as related in the twenty-fourth chapter of the Book of Exodus. A word is first announced: "Moses came to the people and related all the words and ordinances of the Lord." And action follows immediately: "Having sent certain young men of the Israelites to offer sacrifice . . . Moses took half of the blood and put it in large bowls; the other half he splashed on the altar. . . . Then he took the blood and sprinkled it on the people." And the word of God and the sacrificial action engenders a religious response: "Taking the book of the Lord [Moses], read it aloud to the people,

who answered, 'All the Lord has said we will heed and do' "
(Ex. 24:7).

Sacrifice has issued in obedient love of God. In this effort,
man's outlook on the world is set in order, his creative life
is purified, and he is led gently toward a future marked by
intensified consciousness. "We will do all the Lord has commanded." Man has freely responded to God's will, at last.
And submitting to his creaturehood in a religious response,
man enters his community once more as a responsible creative agent.

But that newly won sense of identity implies a death as its
preliminary. Man must see himself in the image of the slain
animal. And in that death, solemnly blessed, he understands
the truth that he also must undergo a death in order to serve
God. Without death he cannot preserve the covenant in his
heart. But in the image of sacrifice, he takes heart to put to
death courageously, day after day, whatever would strike
out against the Love of God. And by these constant new beginnings, dramatized at sacrifice, he learns that his service of
God is no angelic or automatic response-to-value; that only
by an interior metanoia will he come to be God's man.

For the will to serve God must combat mysterious and
massive areas of man's psychology. If it is true to say that
man is naturally religious, in the sense that all that is best in
religious life finds a prior disposition in him—still it must
be admitted that man is naturally pagan too. He wishes to
be himself, at the price even of God and the neighbor. An
imperious instinct tells him that only by honoring and ex-
alting his ego will he be himself at all.

Only a very fond Christian would conclude that this temptation is peculiar to paganism. The saints know better. They see that man attains sonship of God only at the price of the death of selfishness. They know that pride is the name of man which pleases man most of all. It pleases him instinctively, and some men it pleases deliberately—they set about proving the name is rightfully theirs.

But how is sacrifice related to the correction of pride? In its genuine form, sacrifice is the master-drama of man's creaturehood. Man is himself most fully at the community rite. Even the phrase "is himself" is hardly accurate; it smacks of definition rather than of life. In fact, the drama of sacrifice shows man to himself in a most full-blooded and realistic way. It brings to bear upon him the weight of an accepted past, the present moment made sacred; and at the same time, it is an entrance-rite into destiny. And it places man firmly in his universe. It beckons the community to his side; it gathers the material world as instrument of his worship, and so leads him gently and obliquely to a religious use of life—the life of time, of material things, and of the community.

So the hieratic rite—sacred, traditional and manly—brings man into a more creaturely stance. He cannot be at the altar, and be himself, and still be in revolt or isolated or neutral. He brings with him his family, his work, his creative hopes, all the ingredients of life. Like the robe of the priest, life itself streams toward the altar: the life of the home, money-making, childbearing, sickness, poverty—all we name man's life. Man comes and offers not merely the symbolic gifts—a bit of bread and wine—but himself.

If he acts sincerely, he cannot but be transformed by this holy commerce. He is different as man, when he descends

the altar into life once more. The deliberate placing of himself into right relation with the Creator, with his brothers,
and with his cosmos, will distinguish his future choices. He
will be found at any point of crisis, God's man—recognizable
as one who stood at the altar and pronounced words by
which he must abide, or resign his claim to manhood.

It is true, of course, that any present moment has meaning only in relation to the consciousness of man. Outside
him, there is no sense in speaking of the meaning of the moment, since in irrational creation every moment is like every
other. The mark of the passage of time in the cosmos is not
a succession of spiritual choices but only the irresistible
cycle of decline and growth. But in man, the present has
validity; within it, man expresses his existence in choice and
knowledge, in impressing his nature on the material world,
and in furthering his destiny before God. And perhaps his
deepest "present" is summed up in his choice to love and
through his love to accept the life of God and of man into
his existence.

So in the highest sense, no moment for man is like any
other moment. And this uniqueness of each moment is actually heightened by the life of faith. For at each instant—believing man has the opportunity of accepting once more the
living content of his faith—both God and the community
of man. So every instant of time becomes a new enrichment
of his being, and a new perspective of the destiny into which
the gracious God has called him.

And this self-consciousness has a surrounding radiance
which tends to include the consciousness of every other man.
The past of men lives on in the holy choice of the moment;
and this is true especially at worship, when the believer sum-

mons the holy ones of all history to witness the truth of his present—of what he says and does now. "John and Paul, Cosmos and Damian . . . Lucy and Agatha."

Now this intense power of choice that makes time a true "present" to man is not merely a generally heightened awareness. In sacrifice, man does not merely face time and this world aware, in a diffused or vague sense, of being himself. Rather, his spiritual powers assert themselves, in full vigor, to meet a given moment, and within it to express in the widest and richest way possible all that God is, all that man is, all that his race is in him. Man chooses on behalf of existence; he accepts the shape of life as it takes form within him.

The present moment, when expressed in this way, is both disciplined and free. Aware of himself as acting in time and space, the believer is at the same time independent of these. At his center, he knows himself as being both creature and free instrument. And at sacrifice, both these poles of awareness are enlightened and gently corrected. Sacrifice, that is, guards man from the temptation of pride, a revolt against existence and the shape it bears; and on the other hand, it saves him from despair, the temptation of plunging into non-being. It guards man from the will to be God, and the will not to be at all.

But these corrections of life exist, so to speak, at the penumbra of sacrifice. They define the boundaries within which man acts. At the center is the substance of man's encounter with God; the invitation to enter more deeply into sonship, and into the community of man.

Nor is this all. For man is also a material being. His present therefore includes his world. Moreover, in him all creation is made present both to himself and to God. The natural cycles and the material universe that seem to provide no more than a serviceable universe for man, achieve in man's consciousness their highest dignity—they become a parable of the divine will-to-share. They are not, merely neutral objects; they are gifts of God. And this inner "eloquence" of creation is clarified in the sacrificial act, where man frees material objects from the imprisonment of their universe and its time process, and offers them in the praise and gratitude of a liturgical being.

But it is not only symbolic objects which are freed by sacrifice from the slavery of time. Man also has part in this freedom; he is assured a measure of relief from irrational duration. It would be helpful to recall, in this regard, that in pagan religions the cosmic cycles existed only to remind man of the unending decline and birth of all things, including himself. All things were a parable of change. In this view, man was not related to the material world by way of contrast and transcendence; he was only the eloquent voice which mourned and rejoiced for the passing away of all things.

It was because of this deadly reliance on the world of nature as image of all reality that Greek religion fell away. Since it understood the material world as the source from which even the gods sprang, sacrifice could be nothing else than the offering of the cyclic wheel to the imprisoned divinities. There could be no freedom here, divine or human. Rather, a reliance on irrational nature, as image and source of reality, subjected men and gods alike to the wheel of duration. In this way the material world and its eons won out as the measure of reality—to the degree, really, where all things were slaves to process, to birth and decline.

But in Jewish and Christian sacrifice, a radically different view of reality is at work. The world of nature is subject
to a superior order of things. Sacrifice announces a moment
when the cycles of time, and the animals and crops and men
upon their wheel, are led into a new existence. They are in-
gathered by man, who steps outside their fate to command
and use, and in this way asserts his kingly independence of
nature. Man raises them before the All-High to express his
own destiny, and that of his universe—a destiny which man
himself sums up—the Face of the Father.

Sacrifice also has great things to say in regard to man's
future. We could define the future as an area of existence
which is available to man only in an obscure way by some
intuitive process or by prophecy or revelation. In contrast
with his insecure grasp on his future, man truly possesses
his past, and if he is largely human, he possesses something
of the past of all men. And in regard to the present, he not
only possesses it but defines it to the degree that he actually
gives it form by his intelligence and choices, by his imposi-
tion of order on it. But the future is an unknown. And its
obscurity weighs upon man. It burdens him not merely because the future is nonexistent—that state of things can be
borne with, since the future may lie at such distance from
his concern as to seem remote and unrelated to him. And if
he is Christian, his faith bids him center his attention not on
the future, but on "the day" and its sufficiency.

But what man really fears today is that the circumstances
of his world conspire to place the future beyond his grasp in
an altogether violent and brutal way. His foreboding even
tells him that material force threatens his world with disin-

tegration, and that any serious provision for a future is absurd. In this way, by a sort of traumatic dread, man's sense of providence and hope are assaulted.

Now so ominous a sense of the future cannot leave man's present unaffected. In extreme cases, fears centering about the future may reduce man's present to such a point of despair that he simply cannot act. He becomes fixed in obsessive dread, his attention centered upon a monstrous shape taking form before his eyes, omnivorous and brutal.

We are closer perhaps to defining the sense of the future proper to man today. It is not merely that he does not know what shape the future will bear. For as life advances in complexity and the community discovers new and more intricate sub-forms, life itself tends to become less predictable. But this too can be accepted as long as man is still enclosed in the protective tissue of community life, and his fellow men remain eager to shelter him within the life-forms which have always nourished the family of man.

But the case has altered now. Man senses, and with reason, that the future has been stolen from him and from his community. The traditional human groupings, local, rooted, available with their sympathy and friendship, have been weakened by divergent currents of passion—money-getting, the will to power and autonomy, preoccupation with mastery over the mysteries of nature. Some at least of these currents, which formerly were channeled and ordered by community life, are now out of control. They no longer concentrate upon the needs of man or avert to his choices—they are totally indifferent to man. The delicate spiritual equilibrium in which men once existed together, and walked in a common direction, is thus thrown off. The result is a future whose shape is no longer a mystery, but an ugly enigma.

Formerly, the future of man had been conceived in religious terms. Men called it a mystery of Providence. It veiled sorrows for which strength had not yet been granted, and cast man's hope upon God's merciful love. Man, said the parable, was forbidden to gather manna beyond the needs of the day. And whatever fears would rise in him were calmed by the assurance of faith; his needs were written in a Mind and Heart that noted with gentle care the fall of the sparrow, the grasses that flourished for an hour. An exquisitely ordered cosmos was upborne by the loving kindness of Providence, and was held by that same Hand before the regard of man. He could read there the presence of a Love which could not but save and hold him fast.

Believing men will recall, of course, that creation bears the same providential meaning for them today. It is the same meaning, and yet how profoundly altered, and altered by man himself! And the change amounts to this—the world, formerly so simple and tranquil a being, ordered and sustained in its processes by a loving Providence, is no longer simply a divine text; it has become a human one as well. It does not speak now only of God's power; or let us say, it speaks of that power in a way which illumines the power of man as well.

All this is true, and to deny it would be to deny the evidence of one's own eyes. Man is in process of creating a future to his own image. He does not feel with the impact of man even a brief century ago, the immediate pressure of material needs; the need of tranquil weather for his crops, the protection of his family in their flimsy houses, the prayers against dangers encountered in primitive travel.

All this amounts to a great onset of adulthood in man. In a true sense, it should be said that his prayer of petition is no longer that of a child. It is that of a man who prays now to a provident God with a new sense of adulthood, a new sense of his material universe, a more penetrating and inward understanding of nature as parable.

Man's prayer always tends to reflect the state of his life. It cannot do otherwise, indeed, and still be true to man. If men are by and large at a subsistence level of life, then their prayer will reflect their childlike sense of utter dependence on the God of nature. They will look to Him to control and subdue in man's favor those forces over which man himself is powerless.

But man today, except in primitive areas, must be true to a new situation. His life now indicates that he has taken in hand the forces of nature and subdued them, often with great brilliance and ingenuity. And so his prayer of petition, and his sacrificial expression of this, is free to move in a more reflective direction. He is invited really to ask for a new understanding of the spiritual realities that underly his affluence. His prayer of petition, and his understanding of sacrifice, ought to move in the direction of a new and adult sense of sovereignty, of a penetrating of the ironies and depths of such realities as creaturehood and kingship, as the interpenetration of history and eternity, as the fate of the material world in its relation to eternity. His prayer should be that he be spared both the danger of pride and the danger of Christian cowardice, before the new world that Providence is inviting man to.

We have here perhaps a more sophisticated and adult view of sacrifice, as it would illuminate the future of man. The symbols of the altar remain what they have always been —lowly, serviceable, even primitive; a little portion of wine and bread. But their meaning in the rite is the same as it has always been, even while that meaning is more radiant and filled with human implication than ever before.

The future is still, at its deepest, a mystery of love. The God of history is still shaping history. Only now He is doing it with a new invitation issued to the adult race which is in process of claiming its rightful, creaturely, rational kingship over the world.

The future is thus at root no other than it has ever been. And yet it is different, from the point of view of man's part in it. He no longer stands as the empty-handed suppliant before God, filled with awe of natural forces, dependent in an altogether childish sense upon the God of Love for his "daily bread." But his need is nonetheless real for all this. It is a need for that which the bread and wine have always stood, at root. It is a need of freedom from guilt and pride, from sin and the state of sin. It is for the recovery and strengthening of that sense of sonship without which man can never hope to be himself.

The future, we can say, is still a mystery of divine bounty and providence; but it is a mystery in which man may enter with a new confidence and a new intelligence. This is a world whose choices will bring time closer to its consummation, and men nearer their human perfection in Christ.

And sacrifice, finally, reminds men of all this. In Christian sacrifice it is the "return of the Lord" which is heralded. The Lord of Glory enters time, under the sign of sacrifice, and secretly, in humiliation, in the bodies and souls of all— of defeated men and women, of those who are without recourse in this world—in these, He shapes a future to His own will.

Christians must not allow issues to be confounded, or the truth to be submerged by the selfish or destructive or arbitrary rationale of this world. The truth remains firmly evident: man has been granted a knowledge of the future which is sufficient for his needs. The rest is mercy.

But this knowledge which faith grants is a dark one. It is open only before believers; and among them, it makes no concessions to the superficial or the merely curious. It summons the faithful, not the superstitious. It remains sternly silent before those who come seeking signs and portents. But for the sake of the believer, it renews the death-victory of the Son of God, and announces His return to claim for Himself the world for which He died and rose again.

This community action of sacrifice, summing up man's hope and giving it a divine assurance of fulfillment, rejects sternly all trafficking with the occult, with dubious prediction, with the unknowable. The Holy Sacrifice would even imply that if Christians persist in these forbidden games, they become incapable of faith. The center of their religious life falls apart into dubious areas of speculation and rumor. To all intents, they join with those who place their hope in "the things which are seen."

But sacrifice tells the man of faith everything his faith will seek to know. It does this not only by proclaiming one or another aspect of the saving Word but, at the climax of its action, by making present the Love which having saved, does not abandon. And this Love is victorious; it invites man to its own victory, which is His: "Come, and sit at My side on My throne, as I have conquered, and do sit on My Father's throne" (Apoc. 3:21).